Ageless Faith

WISDOM FOR OVERCOMING
TODAY'S CHALENGES

Rick and Jane McKinney

THE ROAD LESS TRAVELED PUBLICATIONS

Copyright

Copyright © 2024 by Rick and Jane McKinney

All rights reserved.

No portion of this book may be reproduced in any form without written permission from the publisher or authors, except as permitted by U.S. copyright law.

Contents

Introduction 1

Pots and Pans 7
MAKING ROOM FOR THE MIRACLE

Against All Odds 15
FACING YOUR GIANTS

Needed: One Big Miracle! 24
DEALING WITH LIONS

Fire and Rain 33
PRAYING DOWN HEAVEN

Sink or Swim 42
OVERCOMING THE OBSTACLES

Queen for a Day 51
RESTING IN GOD'S ARRANGEMENTS

Snake in the Grass 60
LOOKING UP FOR HELP

Finishing Strong 69
ENJOYING GOD'S GRACE

An Empty Cradle 78
BELIEVING EVEN THOUGH

Muddy Water 87
OBEYING GOD'S INSTRUCTIONS

God Has a Bear 95
 KNOWING GOD'S GOT IT

A Fish Story 104
 REPENTING AFTER A FALL

Tunnel Vision 113
 DIGGING DOWN DEEP

Saved By Thorns 122
 TRUSTING HIS PROVISION

A Salt-Free Diet 131
 RESISTING TEMPTATION

Who's in the Trees 140
 LISTENING TO GOD'S VOICE

Final Thoughts 148
A Favor to Ask 151
About the Authors 153

Forward

What do you do when God asks you to walk twenty miles a day from California to Washington DC? Well, if you are like Rick and Jane McKinney, you walk! When I first heard of Rick and Jane's journey across America, I knew I wanted to interview them on my Wholehearted radio show on Christian Mix 106.

Within minutes, I learned that this 3000-mile walk was not Rick and Jane's first act of obedience, but one of a number of countless daily choices they have made to say "yes" to God. Their ministry has led them around the world. Whether planting churches, performing concerts, traveling from village to village, serving as educators, or earning several graduate degrees, Rick and Jane live a life that introduces us to the heart of Jesus and the beauty of an ageless faith - one that reminds us how the act of saying "yes" holds the power to impact the lives of many.

In their words, "We should not expect the path of faith to be smooth and comfortable. We live in a fallen world, prone to sickness, disease, disappointments, and difficulties. But there is one guarantee that can sustain you. And that is His presence."

Ageless Faith truly does provide godly wisdom for overcoming today's challenges while also teaching us to have an expectant heart, one that is prepared to receive God's blessings, one that reminds us of His powerful presence. The authors incorporate scripture, quotes, and exercises that are both relatable and thought-provoking.

After devouring the gifts of wisdom and hope woven together throughout these pages, I found myself expecting and praying for something more - fire and rain to fall from Heaven. It left me reflecting on the words Jesus spoke to the two blind men in Matthew, Chapter 9: "Do you believe that I can do this?" I thought I did, but did I? Did I believe? Did I doubt or simply forget? Sometimes, the weight of the world can press heavily on our shoulders. The gravity of the situations we face can tend to pull us down, but Ageless Faith reminds us that we have a God who can defy gravity, one who can part the seas and walk on water.

If you would like to strengthen your faith and be refreshed in the depths of your soul, I would encourage you to read Ageless Faith.

Jenny Muscatell

Author and Radio Host at Christian Mix 106

Introduction

In 2006, my wife, Jane, and I had the most amazing, once-in-a-lifetime adventure imaginable. We literally walked from one side of the country to the other: 2770 miles! It was a unique call of God to share our faith and pray for our nation. The stories written on our hearts will last a lifetime, and some of the people we met were changed for all eternity when they professed Christ and chose to follow Him.

Throughout the six-month journey, we often commented that we should write a book about all the spiritually significant lessons we learned as we walked. The insights we gained from relatively ordinary events and observations were anything but ordinary. We often laughed and said, "There's a sermon in that."

In our first book, "And...So We Walked," we tried to weave many of those lessons into the storyline. However, as the years have passed since the walk, we have found that the relevance of those lessons has only increased. In addition, we have also been thrilled to see how God has tied them together with the narrative of Scripture.

I (Rick) started teaching Old Testament at the University of the Cumberlands a few years ago. I hate to admit it, but even after preaching and pastoring for fifty years and having three graduate-level degrees, I learned much more those first few semesters than my students. The richness of the story of God's relationship with humankind before the coming of Christ is fascinating.

This book is a result of both the journey across America and my Old Testament studies. God has woven the insights from walking with Him for almost three thousand miles with the wisdom gained from the Hebrew Bible's miraculous and factual accounts into a stunningly beautiful tapestry for living a victorious and miracle-filled life through persevering faith. Even though some of these stories are millennia old, they still provide relevant truth for today. This is ageless faith.

What we have observed over many years in the ministry together is that some people's faith is short-lived. Jesus told the parable about seeds sown in different kinds of soil. Some of the seeds sprout but die quickly. Others live a while but wilt when the conditions aren't ideal for growth—only a few flourish. Faith can have a similar life cycle. We fear many today are "selling" a pie-in-the-sky kind of religion that insinuates that life is a bed of roses. When that doesn't happen, people tend to throw in the towel and give up. In many situations, the Church as a whole lacks a balanced kind of discipleship that prepares believers for tough times while teaching them the importance of faith that can withstand the storms of life.

My wife (Jane) says I'm an eternal optimist. I tend to always see hope for the future instead of disaster. This book will reflect that hope. But you should also know that the spiritual lessons and principles contained in these pages will assume that we will all go through some tough times. The question is: Can the Bible help us discover how to live an abundant life full of God-sized events that will cause people to say, like those who saw fire fall from heaven on Mt. Carmel, "Indeed, this is the One, True God?" And can that happen even in times of hardship, trial, and difficulties? Yes, without a doubt.

But please understand what we are not saying. This

is not a "name-it-and-claim-it," positive thinking, "everything's gonna be alright" book. This book will not reprimand you for not having enough faith. We're not going to insinuate that the problems you face result from divine judgment. As you will see in the following pages, bad things sometimes happen to good people. When they do, faith can carry you through. We hope you will see that the quantity of your faith is not nearly as important as the quality of your faith.

I'd love to write a book outlining three easy steps to always get what you pray for; it's just not that simple. Living a life of faith that stands when times get tough can be complicated. Sometimes, there are no easy answers; look at the story of Job. Those who teach and preach that there are ways to guarantee green traffic lights and close-to-the-door parking spaces should consider that the most outstanding, faith-filled people in the Bible endured incredibly difficult times. Sometimes, regardless of how close to God you are, life will crumble around you and leave you standing in a pile of rubble.

Faith must be exercised even when the world is falling apart. We must learn to stand in faith, even when the debt collector is knocking at the door, or the flood waters are about to break the dam. We should not expect the path of faith to be smooth and comfortable. We live in a fallen world, prone to sickness, disease, disappointments, and difficulties. Even so, we hope by reading this book, you will be encouraged not to give up or give in. Walking in faith is not a cakewalk. There are times when it's more like walking on a bed of hot coals. Somedays are downright grueling. But there is one guarantee that can sustain you. And that is his presence.

> Be strong and courageous. Do not
> fear or be in dread of them, for it is the
> LORD your God who goes with you.
> He will not leave you or forsake you."

Deuteronomy 31:6 ESV

We're glad you're reading this book. Reliving the stories of Scripture and getting reacquainted with the ordinary people who became heroes of our faith can fill us with heavenly hope. Rest assured; God will also work through you when you have faith that stands the test of time.

Rick and Jane McKinney

Pots and Pans

Pots and Pans

MAKING ROOM FOR THE MIRACLE

Expecting an Outpouring

In 2005, when Jane and I began to prepare for our cross-country walk, we had decisions to make. As we started purchasing clothes, shoes, rain gear, and even non-perishable food for the six-month journey, we had to decide whether or not to prepare in faith for the entire walk (nearly 3000 miles) or wait to see if we would last that long.

Faith said, "Prepare for the entire trip. With God's help, you'll make it." Doubt said, "Don't waste all the money. You may only be able to walk a couple hundred miles. Then you'll be stuck with a truckload of supplies you don't need." Faith was on one shoulder and doubt on the other. The question was ominous. Which one should we listen to, common sense or uncommon faith?

It seemed to us that preparing for the whole journey was a signal to God and others that we believed we would receive an outpouring of God's supernatural strength, power, and perseverance to walk from one coast to the other. Preparing for less would be a confession we did not think we would finish. So, using our best calculations, we purchased what would be needed for the entire trip.

A poignant narrative in the Bible points to this kind of faith. Here are a few verses from that story:

> 5 So she went from him and shut the door behind her and her sons, who brought the vessels to her; and she poured it out.
>
> 6 Now it came to pass, when the vessels were full, that she said to her son, "Bring me another vessel." And he said to her, "There is not another vessel." So, the oil ceased.
>
> 7 Then she came and told the man of God. And he said, "Go, sell the oil and pay your debt, and you and your sons live on the rest."
>
> II Kings 4:5-7 NKJV

This story has always intrigued me. It is a bona fide miracle. A widow with no resources of her own, destitute by all standards, and about to lose her sons to debtors-slavery, comes to the prophet Elisha with her impossible-looking situation. She not only had no oil but didn't even have pots and pans to hold oil if she had any.

Now, here's what's interesting. Elisha did not instruct her to borrow oil. She would have increased her debt by owing her neighbors for the oil if she had done that. Instead, she was told to borrow the vessels that would hold the miracle oil. There are several lessons to be gleaned. One, God does not need our resources to produce a miracle. Neither the pots nor the oil were part of the widow's possessions. Remember, God created the universe out of nothingness. He doesn't need raw materials to start with. He is the raw material. I love it when we are worshipping God in a corporate setting, and God moves on my heart to offer my empty hands to him in praise. Essentially, I am saying, "God, all I can offer you is empty hands, but I trust that you will fill them with whatever I need to fulfill your calling on my life."

Two, God's plan (always best) allowed her to sell the oil for enough to pay her debts and then return the empty pots to her neighbors, owing them nothing but her gratitude. We do not need to go into debt to help God out. As someone said, "Where God guides, He provides." We sometimes contaminate the extraordinary by compromising it with the ordinary. Supernatural miracles don't need to be propped up with our naturally obtained resources or abilities.

Although I rarely have time, I love to cook. When I see a tempting recipe, I want to get the ingredients and prepare it. Usually, I do pretty well, and the meal is delicious. However, I tend to want to experiment. Sometimes, as I add ingredients not listed in the recipe, instead of enhancing the dish, it ruins it. The person who published the recipe has likely already tried many variations and concluded that this is the perfect blend. Adding our own "stuff" just ruins what would otherwise be a perfect meal. The same is true when we try to enhance God's recipe for an abundant life.

Three, and this is the best part, the only limitations to the size of her miracle were her obedience and the largeness of her vision. She didn't have to own anything. She simply had to obey. And here's the key: The size of the miracle was determined entirely by the depth of her faith. By and large, we expect too little from God. We're not sure He's able. After all, people think, "He is getting old and perhaps a bit feeble." Fortunately, this is not true. He is the same yesterday, today, and forever. His presence, power, or preferences have not changed.

What is the Size of Your Expectation?

Elisha did not tell her how many pots to borrow. That was left up to her and her expectation of God's provision. What if she had borrowed one more pot, five or even ten? Those pots would have been filled with oil, too, right? What does that mean for us? The principle is the same. If my expectation for God's provision is small, it will limit the size of the miracle. Please understand that this is not God punishing us for not having more faith. It is simply that God will only give us what we are prepared to receive and steward well.

The Perfect Illustration

When serving my first church as their youth pastor, I had an experience that will always remind me of this principle. I had composed a contemporary musical for our youth choir to perform. To put it mildly, the pastor was not one of my biggest fans. It wasn't just me; he liked very few people. He had reluctantly agreed to allow us to take the Sunday evening service to present it for the first time. The choir worked hard, not only on the musical but also on inviting their friends and classmates to the event. On Sunday afternoon, the pastor and I met at the church office to run off programs on the old mimeograph machine. He asked me how many copies I thought we should make. He suggested 50. The worship center held about 200 people, and the youth prayed for weeks for a packed house. I enthusiastically suggested 200. He literally laughed in my face. We talked, actually he talked, telling me how foolish I was being. He chalked it up to my youth (I was only 18) and inexperience. He finally agreed to run 200. I think he planned to show me all the wasted leftover programs at the night's end. When the "curtain went up," the building was packed. It was standing room only. It was one of the highlights of my ministry. The Spirit of God moved, and people responded to the invitation to follow Jesus, including one student whom the students had been earnestly praying would come to Christ. What would have happened if we had printed only 50 copies? I believe we would have had enough people for the programs...50! To put it another way, just enough oil to fill the pots!

> Consider this: God did not give her more because the oil would have spilled and been wasted. God will not give you more than you are prepared to receive. So, expect big! Plan to receive big and manage what He blesses you with well. Then next time, He will trust you with even more. (This is the principle taught in the Parable of the Talents)

High expectations are the key to everything.

Sam Walton

How can you make room in your life for God's miraculous supply?

Do you have the faith to step out and make it obvious you are expecting a blessing?

Are you willing to face ridicule from others because you are expecting something God-sized? Make two lists.

On one side of the page, list the miracles you are praying for in your life.

On the other side of the page, list how you are preparing to receive God's provision."

II Kings 4:5-7 NKJV

Against All Odds

Against All Odds

FACING YOUR GIANTS

Standing Tall

During the year of preparation for the walk, we had discussions with several people who had made long-distance walks. We even met with one walker just finishing his walk across America on Route 66. He actually invited us to walk with him for the final five miles of his journey. After he took his last few steps, he turned to the newspaper reporter who was there to document the conclusion of his walk; he introduced us and said, "I'm passing the torch on to these two folks." It was an extraordinary moment in time.

As we walked, we had dozens of questions for him, but one seemed most pressing. We asked timidly, almost not wanting to know, "What was your biggest obstacle or problem?" Dennis didn't hesitate, "Dogs. Absolutely, it was dogs." Now, this was especially concerning to me because I've always had a fear of dogs I don't know. I was chased by a pack of dogs when I was a young boy walking home from school, and it scarred me for life.

We didn't have to walk many days to see that Dennis was right. We encountered dogs all the way across America. A few were friendly, but most saw us as a potential chew toy. One afternoon in Tennessee, we saw a beautiful home with hundreds of feet of white fence surrounding the property. There was a long driveway from the house to the street. We noticed a car coming down the lane toward the highway and a large Doberman Pinscher running behind it. It seemed apparent that the owner was leaving, and the dog had been left in charge.

Usually, if the dog's owner was home, they would stick their head out of the front door and call the dog inside. But the owner was gone in this instance, and this dog was massive. It spotted us and started barking and coming toward the street. What could we do? I pulled myself up as tall as possible, looked the dog in the face, and shouted, "In the name of Jesus, STOP and go home!" Honest, the dog whimpered, turned around, and ran back down the driveway toward home.

I know a Doberman isn't quite like a nine-foot giant, but I wonder if that's a little how David felt as He listened to Goliath ridicule the army of God.

> 8 He stood and shouted to the ranks of Israel and said to them, "Why do you come out to draw up in battle array? Am I not the Philistine and you servants

> of Saul? Choose a man for yourselves
> and let him come down to me.
>
> 9 If he is able to fight with me and kill
> me, then we will become your servants;
> but if I prevail against him and kill him,
> then you shall become our servants and
> serve us."
>
> I Samuel 17:8-9 NASB95

Numerous accounts in the Old Testament recount the Israeli army being outnumbered only to carry out a victorious campaign. Sometimes, they were outmanned by tens of thousands. Gideon's victory over the Midianites is one example of God providing a miraculous victory against unbelievable odds.

But perhaps there is no more dramatic illustration of this than that of David and Goliath. David, a young shepherd inexperienced in the nuances of warfare, refused to allow the taunts of the Philistine Goliath to go unchallenged. Dwarfed by a giant nearly twice his size, he marched into the valley of Elah, armed with three things: a sling, five smooth stones, and memories of how the God of Israel had empowered him when fighting wild animals that threatened his flock.

You probably know the end of the story. David's skillfully slung stone renders Goliath unconscious, allowing him to decapitate his rival and fulfill the prophetic words he had spoken just a short time earlier.

> 45 Then David said to the Philistine, "You come to me with a sword, a spear, and a javelin, but I come to you in the name of the Lord of hosts, the God of the armies of Israel, whom you have taunted.
>
> 46 This day, the Lord will deliver you up into my hands, and I will strike you down and remove your head from you."
>
> I Samuel 17:45-46 NASB95

I don't know which is more challenging, believing God for the miraculous provision of oil or defeating a giant. But I do know this: they are both miracles and require faith that God can do the impossible. Both necessitate a kind of deep confidence that God is able, whether you're standing in the middle of the valley of the shadow of death or fighting back the doubt that comes when facing the angry bill collectors.

My experience, and I believe it aligns with Scripture, is that we learn to exercise faith in little things first. God rarely requires us to face the "Goliaths" right off the bat. Faith is built up like a muscle, a bit each day. Don't despise the small experiences that teach you small faith. Those times will spur you on to face more substantial challenges, and your faith will grow to overcome them all. When rebuilding the temple, Zerubbabel, discouraged by the delay in the completion of the project, was admonished by God: "Do not despise these small beginnings, for the Lord rejoices to see the work begin, to see the plumb line in Zerubbabel's hand" (Zechariah 4:10). Did you catch that? God delights in small steps of faith. Take the first one and then the next. This is how you build your resume of faith.

One Small Step At a Time

There were days, many days, when we did not know how we could walk another step. Our feet were so blistered and raw that we could barely put shoes and socks on. But time after time, we would say to each other, "just take the next step". When we look back on those six months, we're still not sure how we made it, except that God rejoiced in seeing two of His children continue to take obedient steps. Every morning, as we headed out toward our starting point, we remembered that God had been faithful the day before, and we were confident He would be faithful that day as well.

> He didn't bring us this far to leave us
>
> He didn't teach us to swim to let us drown
>
> He didn't build His home in us
>
> to move away
>
> He didn't lift us up to let us down
>
> Phil Johnson

Do You Have a History with God?

Notably, David drew on his past experiences to bolster his faith in a God who can deliver in the most challenging circumstances. What about you? Do you have a history with the miraculous God? Perhaps He came through during a financial crisis with provision. Remember that time when you could have been injured or even killed, and God's protective hand kept you from harm? What about when God touched you and restored you to health? Every single child of God has a collection of these kinds of memories. Now, leverage them into the faith needed to stand tall, straight, and fearlessly as you face the giant threatening to steal your joy, livelihood, family, or peace of mind. Declare with David, "This day, the Lord will deliver me and give me the victory!"

Jane and I have spent half a century assembling a "spiritual photo album" of all the miraculous ways God has intervened in our lives. Sometimes, we were rescued. Other times, we were given protection or provision. The miracles came in all different sizes and shapes. But we kept track. From time to time, when we are going through a difficult time, we pull out the photo album and remind each other of all the ways God has seen us through. He has never forsaken us. He has always been faithful, and He always will be!

> **Consider this: Each memory of past victories serves as one rung on the ladder of faith. Every future victory will be won by standing on the foundation built using past miracles as the building blocks. Don't minimize past victories and regard them as insignificant. Please don't allow yourself to forget them. Remember them... thank God for them...then turn and face today with the confidence that the same God who delivered David will deliver you.**

Gratitude makes sense of our past, brings peace for today, and creates a vision for tomorrow.
Melody Beattie

Make a list of past blessings, victories, and miracles in your life that are reasons for believing that more is on the way.

If you are more of a visual person, you may want to make your own scrapbook. Put pictures or mementos that will remind you of God's goodness.

Beside each of the events you listed, write a few thoughts describing what you learned about the nature of God from that experience. How do each of those lessons bolster your faith today?

Needed: One Big Miracle

Needed: One Big Miracle!

DEALING WITH LIONS

Outrunning Trains

There were several places in Arizona where Route 66 was non-existent. Once the Interstate was built, many short sections outside the bigger towns were bulldozed. This wasn't usually a problem since, in most locations, we had been permitted to walk on the Interstate when necessary.

However, in Arizona, several huge canyons were spanned by Interstate bridges with no shoulder. We just didn't feel safe walking several hundred feet with nowhere to go when a semi barreled past at 70 m.p.h. So, when we discovered such a situation while scouting out the route the night before, we'd try to find the closest railroad tracks to walk on.

Of course, the railroad tracks had to cross those same canyons. The advantage was there were fewer trains than trucks. Sometimes, the train trestles were nearly a quarter-mile long. We would feel the tracks to see if they vibrated (meaning a train was coming). If not, we would pray, take a deep breath, and run. If we were wrong, it meant either getting hit by a train or jumping to a certain death. Neither were great choices.

We only had to do this two or three times. Once, a train passed us about five minutes after crossing the canyon. It was a situation where we would have died if God hadn't come through. This was a situation that had the potential to take our lives, but we were sure that God would be faithful and protect us...and He did.

I think Daniel was sure, too. He knew he was being obedient and faithful to God and believed that God would be faithful to him. That is the kind of faith that stands the test of time. Before we took our first steps in Santa Monica, California, we had decided that we'd rather die being obedient than live in disobedience. Daniel had made the same decision.

We used to sing a little chorus quite a bit entitled, "Turn Your Eyes Upon Jesus." I love the last half of the refrain that says, "And the things of earth will grow strangely dim, In the light of His glory and grace." That's it! When you look into His face, everything else fades: Trains, trucks, dogs, and even lions!

> 16 Then the king gave orders, and Daniel was brought in and cast into

the lions' den. The king spoke and
said to Daniel, "Your God whom you
constantly serve will Himself deliver
you."

17 A stone was brought and laid over
the mouth of the den, and the king
sealed it with his own signet ring and
with the signet rings of his nobles
so that nothing would be changed
regarding Daniel.

Daniel 6:16-17 NASB95

Have you ever been in a situation where you thought, "If God doesn't come through...I'm sunk?" There's no doubt that Daniel must have experienced those thoughts as he was thrown into a den full of hungry lions. As he felt nothing but air under his feet, his prayer might have gone like this: "God, I need one big miracle right now!"

Most of those thrown to the lions never hit the dirt. The ravenous beasts would have torn them to shreds while still in mid-air. That may have been a blessing considering the alternative of the lions playing "cat and mouse" with you as you endured the torturous ordeal. Daniel wasn't in any position to negotiate with the lions. He needed an immediate and decisive miracle. Is that where you are right now, about to be eaten alive by your circumstances?

We are not given much information about Daniel's state of mind. We can surmise that most of us would be fearful beyond words and probably second-guessing our decision to keep praying when we knew it would land us in this frightful situation. But not Daniel. He had resolved to be obedient to God, regardless of the consequences.

It's OK to be Afraid

I do not mean to imply that having this kind of determination removes all fear and trepidation. Being obedient to the call of God upon our lives does not render our human emotions numb to the circumstances around us. As long as we are trapped in this "vessel of clay," our knees will sometimes tremble, we will occasionally sweat bullets, and we may even stand paralyzed with fear as we face the consequences of our obedience.

So how do we face what's ahead, knowing there could be a hungry lion around the next corner? How do we continue to say yes to God, even when the price may be extreme? I believe the answer is found in another story taken from this time period. Shadrach, Meshach, and Abednego faced certain death in the fiery furnace because of their unfailing devotion to God. Their response is astounding when given one last chance to recant and bow down to the idol.

> 17 "If we are thrown into the blazing furnace, the God we serve can deliver us from it, and he will deliver us from Your Majesty's hand.
>
> 18 But even if he does not, we want you to know, Your Majesty, that we will not serve your gods or worship the image of gold you have set up."

Daniel 3:17-18

But What if He Doesn't Come Through?

Our attitude must be the same as that of Daniel and the three Hebrew children. Our resolve, like theirs, must be: We win either way. If God delivers us, we win. If he doesn't, we still win because we didn't bow, and we'll be in God's presence a little sooner than we expected! Paul hints at this in Romans Chapter 8 when he says, "We are more than conquerors in Christ Jesus." We are more than mere winners because, with God, we win regardless. Followers of Jesus are unique. We cannot lose because "To live is Christ and to die is gain" (Phil. 1:21).

It dawned on me one day that for Christians, there is no "worst-case scenario." Most people believe that the worst that can happen in any particular situation is death. That may be the most severe or dramatic consequence, but for a believer, what's better than being welcomed into our heavenly home by our Savior? When you live with that perspective, it changes the abandon with which you live. That doesn't mean you step out in front of moving trains, hoping that God will rescue you. But it does mean that you refuse to live your life in constant fear of the consequences of being sold out to God.

One of the most poignant lessons in these two stories is that there was no disconnect between faith and practice. These four individuals exemplified that faith should not be restricted to the "religious" sector of our lives. It must permeate every hour of every day. Faith must percolate through life's typical "filters" and saturate every nook and cranny.

> Consider this: Our faith must not only work in the church building while singing hymns and listening to the sermon. Our faith MUST work in the lion's den as well. It has to work in the fiery furnace. The "Hall of Faith" in Hebrews 11 reminds us that Abraham's faith worked on Mt. Moriah. Rahab's worked when the walls were crumbling around her. Noah's faith worked with every blow of the hammer while being ridiculed as he built the ark. Will your faith work in a situation that calls for One Big Miracle?

Faith is a living, daring confidence in God's grace, so sure and certain that a man could stake his life on it a thousand times.

Martin Luther

What "lions" are threatening you?

Are you trusting that God can deliver you?

If you were threatened to be thrown into a situation requiring God to come through for your survival, could you stand firm in your belief that God is worth that risk?

What would it take to plant your feet and declare, "I shall not be moved?"

Or, in the famous words of Martin Luther, as he addressed the court that had the power to strip him of his credentials, "Here, I Stand!" Are you convicted of any situations in your life where you need to put your foot down and make a stand? If so, list them here.

Fire and Rain

Fire and Rain

PRAYING DOWN HEAVEN

Prayer Walking

One of the most significant lessons we learned as we walked eight-plus hours every day was about prayer. We jokingly say, "It was the world's longest prayer walk." We don't know for sure if that's true, but one thing we do know: When you walk that long, day after day with the same person, you eventually run out of things to say to each other. On the other hand, you never seem to run out of things to say to God.

We discovered that when your conversations with God take up most of the day, you shed a lot of the "prayer baggage" that most of us seem to carry around when we talk to our Heavenly Father. The formalities are stripped away. The flowery language we tend to use to impress those in the church service fades. The religious idioms are swapped for plain, raw, embarrassingly honest requests that seem to somehow ring true.

I caught myself, especially in the desert, talking softly in heart-felt spurts of spontaneous petitions for those passing by in cars or sitting on their covered porch trying to get some relief from the heat. The prayers were often single words or incomplete sentences, but I was sure God understood. Several times, I found I was repeating one word repeatedly for several minutes. Whatever or whoever was heavy on my heart was prompting me to knock on the Father's door, over and over, asking for the answer. It never seemed unnatural or manufactured. It was just the free-flowing words and phrases of a Spirit-led prayer. This was not the "prayer language" that many describe. But, it certainly was my understandable prayer language that the Spirit of God was prompting.

We learned that God wants us to speak to Him about the honest desires of our hearts. We also discovered the joy of praying for others on a level we had never experienced before. We see these truths affirmed in the beautiful story of Elijah on Mt. Carmel. If you read the story carefully, you will observe two kinds of prayers. On the one hand, we see "religious prayers." On the other, the type of prayer that brings fire and rain.

> 38 Then the fire of the Lord fell and burned up the sacrifice, the wood, the stones, and the soil, and also licked up the water in the trench.
>
> I Kings 18:38NIV

Jane and I grew up in what we believe was the golden age of music, at least pop music. In the late '60s and early '70s, our hearts were stirred by the music of The Beatles, Creedence Clearwater Revival, Pure Prairie League, John Denver, and, of course, James Taylor. We've been privileged to see so many of these artists in concert through the years. One of our favorite memories is hearing James Taylor sing "Fire and Rain" in concert. It was awesome!

As odd as it may seem, a part of me thinks about Elijah every time I hear that song. Actually, the chorus could have been his theme song. His ability to trust God for the miraculous showed itself in several ways. But perhaps two of the most sensational involved fire and rain. His prayer for a drought highlighted God's judgment for the pervasive evil promoted under the reign of Ahab and Jezebel. These two rotten-to-the-core rulers of Israel were despicable. Their hatred for Jehovah God and all that was holy was well-known. Elijah's prayer precipitated the drought and caused those affected by it to look up to the heavens for relief constantly. The return of rain (at Elijah's request) pointed to God's goodness despite the evil that prevailed. The fire that fell from heaven on Mt. Carmel demonstrated that the Lord God, Jehovah, was the one true God.

Both the story of Elijah and our prayer walk illustrate an essential principle of living a miraculous life. We sometimes feel God withholds His supernatural intervention in our lives because our prayers aren't polished enough or theologically correct. But Elijah's requests for God to withhold rain, consume his altar, and sacrifice with fire, then later send rain to the parched land were all brief, concise, and "to-the-point" prayers. There was nothing eloquent about them. They were, in fact, very ordinary prayers that any of us could pray. Similarly, Jane and I saw God answer our straightforward, honest prayers daily as we journeyed across the country with a burden for the salvation of its people.

On the other hand, the priests of Baal had been praying to their god of stone all day, cutting themselves with sharp stones and, no doubt, making a spectacle of themselves. Their long and tedious supplications were ignored. This has often made me wonder, as I've listened to the meticulously crafted, type-written prayers of the pious, whether or not those prayers get any higher than the ceiling. I also tend to pause when I hear someone who is ill at ease in the presence of God. They pray as though they don't know God and He doesn't know them. Both kinds of prayers are a sad reflection of how little intimacy there is between ourselves and our loving Father.

What Impresses God?

God does not answer our prayers because they are long and fancy. He does not honor self-mutilation. Nor is He impressed with any other pretense of self-righteousness and religiosity. He responds to just the opposite. He is moved by a pure heart, an honest faith, and an earnest desire to see God move. This requires a familiarity with who God is. This kind of praying is spurred on by being on a "first name basis" with God. Those in my generation may remember Archie Bunker from the television program "All In The Family." When he prayed, he always gave God his street address so God would remember who he was. The problem wasn't that God didn't know Archie. The issue was that Archie didn't know God. So, before we pray for external miracles, perhaps we should pray for internal, spiritual ones.

> 10 Create in me a clean heart, O God,
>   and renew a right spirit within me.
>
> Psalm51:10 ESV

God sees what's in our hearts. He knows our motivations. He recognizes selfless requests and honors them. He resists the proud and the self-serving prayers they pray. My shallowness was exposed many years ago when I analyzed how many of my own prayers were self-focused. It can be a frightening exercise. If others were to hear our private prayers, would they be repulsed by our self-absorption, or would they be inspired by the simple sincerity of our selfless petitions? Elijah's prayers pointed people upward to the one true God. Ours should, too.

My best guess is that Elijah was a man who kept himself spiritually fit, his heart pure, his motives selfless, and his faith strong. We would do well to follow that pattern. Evaluating our prayer life is a healthy habit. Not in an academic way, but as we might consider any relationship we have. Here is an excellent three-point checklist.

> 1. Let nothing keep you at a distance from God.
> 2. Spend twice as much time praying for others than for yourself.
> 3. Keep track of answered prayers and give God constant praise.

Someone once asked me how long they should pray each day. Here is my best answer. Pray enough for prayer to become the most naturally occurring thing you do each day. Pray enough that your first response to every situation is calling on God. Pray enough that there is peace in your heart that God is handling the problem.

> **Consider this: While many times our prayers are focused toward us, the prayers that bring heaven down are those focused on others. Look out to see the needs of others. Look up to God for the need to be supplied. Look around to see the miraculous answers God will give.**

> Expect to have hope rekindled.
> Expect your prayers to be answered in
> wondrous ways. The dry seasons in life
> do not last. The spring rains will come
> again.
>
> Sarah Ban Breathnach

List the three most pressing needs in the lives of three friends or family members.

Under each one, compose a simple, short prayer that addresses that need. Keep the prayer to fifty words or less.

Write the prayers here, then copy them onto 3X5 cards several times. Place them in the high-traffic areas of your life (car dashboard, bathroom mirror or wall, dining table, etc.).

Each time you see the card, pick it up and pray the prayer. Continue to do this until you see the "fire and rain, fall."

Sink or Swim

Sink or Swim

OVERCOMING THE OBSTACLES

One Step at a Time

Many times during our six-month journey, our bodies screamed, "Quit!" There were mornings when climbing out of bed hurt. Some days, just putting on shoes and socks caused excruciating pain. In the desert, just putting your blistered feet down on the hot, rough pavement of a deteriorating Route 66 caused our legs to recoil in protest. It would have been easy to give up.

But giving up would not only have been disobedient but would have resulted in something far worse. It would have started a domino effect that affected us and thousands of other people who were touched by the walk along the way. We had been praying for a year that God would set up divine appointments, and did He ever. We met and shared the gospel with security guards, DHL delivery drivers, bus riders, pastors, truck drivers, homeless people, restaurant servers, a witch, cashiers in convenience stores, and hundreds more. Had we quit, none of them would have heard the gospel on those days. But if you consider that each of them probably told others about our walk and what we had shared with them, the ripple effect probably touched thousands, if not tens of thousands, of lives!

Every day, God reminded us that our obedience had consequences…that affected many people. Many people feel their obedience to God is a private matter. Nothing could be further from the truth. Every move you make affects other people. Every obedient act impacts the lives of those you sit next to at work, buy gas from at the station, attend social functions with at parties, and live next to in your neighborhood. Every disobedient act also affects them.

Joshua understood this principle. If he obeyed God and crossed the Jordan River, it would affect every man, woman, and child. The promised land was close enough to see but could not be entered without an act of obedience. God wasn't surprised by the presence of the Jordan River. He wasn't surprised by our obstacles either. He knew all the discomfort, pain, and even every blister before we were aware of them. But He also had a plan for us. And he had a plan for Joshua, too.

15 Now, the Jordan is at flood stage, all during harvest. Yet as soon as the priests who carried the ark reached the Jordan and their feet touched the water's edge,

16 the water from upstream stopped flowing. It piled up in a heap a great distance away at a town called Adam in the vicinity of Zarethan, while the water flowing down to the Dead Sea was completely cut off. So the people crossed over opposite Jericho.

Joshua 3:15-16 NASB95

Water is an enigma. It is a paradox of sorts. It can be life-giving. You cannot live without water. But in the wrong circumstances, it can take a life. It can bring

great enjoyment at a swimming pool or water park. It can also destroy towns, houses, and belongings when a river floods over its banks. A gentle rain can give nourishment and refreshment to a farmer's field, but a torrential downpour can beat a potential crop to the ground, and it may not recover.

In Joshua, we read the account of the children of Israel's journey into the Promised Land. In Chapter 3, they encounter an obstacle...water. The Jordan River was at flood stage, which was good because the flooding waters irrigated the fields for miles around. The problem was that it also made it impossible for the crowds of people to cross to the other side.

God is Never Surprised!

Although this circumstance most likely surprised Joshua, it didn't catch God off guard. God saw the obstacle before Joshua and the children of Israel. And here's the amazing thing: God already had a miracle in mind to overcome the obstacle. The good news is that He always does! There is no obstacle, challenge, temptation, or circumstance that God doesn't already have a specific plan in mind to overcome. The God of the universe has already seen every entanglement and difficulty you will ever face in your faith journey. He has a custom-made, gift-wrapped, supernatural miracle in mind to bring deliverance and victory. The miracle may be endurance to make it through. It may be the ability to walk wounded. It may be to crawl across the finish line. And quite frankly, the miracle may be our transport to glory, but there's always a miracle.

> 13 No test or temptation that comes your way is beyond the course of what others have had to face. All you need to remember is that God will never let you down; he'll never let you be pushed past your limit; he'll always be there to help you overcome it.
>
> I Corinthians 10:13 The Message

Please note that God doesn't promise to remove the obstacle. That's always our preference. Most often, the deliverance is THROUGH the obstacle: through the water, floods, and fire. We saw this principle reinforced over and over on our walk across America. Sometimes, we had to cross rushing streams cascading down from the mountains. Other times, we walked with wildfires burning on either side of the road, and the smoke was so thick we could hardly breathe. We walked through some of the most violent and hostile neighborhoods in the nation. Rarely did God direct us around danger. Most often, He said, "Let's go, I'll hold your hand as we walk through it together."

Sometimes, He asks us to walk blindfolded across a great chasm on the thinnest of tightropes. There is an obvious potential for death. But would you walk across if you knew you would arrive safely on the other side? Would you risk it if you knew He was walking beside you? The first step might be tentative. The second is a little more robust. By the time you reach the halfway point, you're skipping, and by the end of your faith walk, you're dancing and doing flip-flops. That's how it is with faith, obedience, and miracles.

> When you pass through the waters, I
> will be with you; and through the rivers,
> they shall not overwhelm you; when
> you walk through the fire, you shall
> not be burned, and the flame shall not
> consume you.
>
> Isaiah 43:2 ESV

The priests kept walking until their feet touched the water. Then, they continued walking into the water. And as they walked, the waters parted. The miracle happened as they walked. There is no indication that they paused, waited, or stopped. They just kept walking. I think a few were doing somersaults by the time they reached the other side! It is difficult to walk through tough times without hesitation, but it can be the key that unlocks the door to victorious living. Sometimes, you can feel the danger, and your brain gives you a dozen reasons not to go forward. But your heart gives you an even bigger one to take another step...obedience.

> Consider this: Obedience is always an ingredient in overcoming. But continuous, consistent obedience (without pausing, waiting, or stopping) is the secret to miraculous living. Don't stop walking when your feet get wet. Don't give up when you feel the heat from the flames. Don't hesitate when you don't see how it will work out. Just keep walking.

This idea of the transcendent power
of the Supreme Being is essentially
connected with that by which the whole
duty of man is summed up: obedience
to His will.

John Quincy Adams

Ask God to reveal any areas where you have been disobedient. Write them down.

Now, one at a time, go through your list and ask God to help you surrender each area of resistance to Him.

Then, get up and DO at least one of those things. Continue to come back to this list and check them off, one by one, as you become obedient in those areas.

Queen for a Day

Queen for a Day
Resting in God's Arrangements

Divine Appointments

There are dozens of stories from the walk across America that affirm the divine appointments that God set up for us. There was Shannon, the young woman who had just broken up with her boyfriend in Albuquerque. Then there was Jeff in Morrilton, Arkansas, Anthony in Los Angeles, the car wash owner in Memphis, and the Navajo men working on their church building in Gallup, New Mexico. Practically every day, we saw God arrange circumstances to put us in the right place at the right time.

We discovered that every stop at a convenience store for a restroom break had been arranged by God. The cashiers were on duty at that particular time so that we could share the love of Jesus with them. It was not happenstance. On those days, they were grieving, troubled, or in some sort of distress. When we walked in, it was obvious that, although they didn't realize it, they were waiting for us to arrive. City workers were repairing broken water mains, which had just "happened" to break just before we arrived in their town. Homeowners in Dickson, Tennessee, had experienced a wind storm the night before and were picking up the limbs and branches from their yards as we walked down the street.

After sharing with people across America, we can't count the number of times the response was something like this: "You two came along at just the right time." Some even said, "I can't believe you showed up today. This is just what I needed to hear today." If you were betting on the odds of us being at particular places at precise times, you would most likely lose the bet every time. These encounters should not have happened, but they did by the hundreds. It shouldn't have been us, the most unlikely cross-country walkers you'll ever meet. We didn't fit the profile. We weren't athletes. We were too old, out of shape, and underfunded. But we were called and placed there for just "such a time."

> 17 And the king loved Esther more than the other young women. He was so delighted with her that he set the royal crown on her head and declared her queen instead of Vashti.
>
> Esther 2:17 NLT

It shouldn't have happened. It wasn't the ordinary course of events. It didn't follow protocol. This is the first time we've seen it done like this. All of these phrases could describe the rise of Esther to the position of Queen. It had never been done like this before. But this book is about miracles and God's desire to use us as conduits for His supernatural work.

Esther was a Jewess. To become the queen of the Persian Empire was something that could only have been orchestrated by the hand of God. Every puzzle piece falls perfectly into place as you read the amazing story. But this is the earmark of a true miracle. God's shadow is cast over the entire narrative. His fingerprints are on every circumstance. The sweet aroma of His presence lingers long after the obstacle is miraculously overcome. An interesting fact about this book and story. Some were unsure about including this book in the Old Testament canon because God is not explicitly mentioned. But His orchestration of the events is unmistakable. The Book of Esther is the story of God without using His name!

The crowning of Esther as queen is only part of the story. It is pivotal, to be sure, but certainly not the most significant regarding the future of the Jewish people. Esther's position as queen gave her access to the King. That's how she was able to derail Haman's plot to exterminate the Jewish people. Think about that. Had God not intervened at this point in history, the Jewish nation could have been eradicated.

God's people had struggled through oppression and captivity and now faced possible extinction. Their problems were mostly of their own making. Their rebellion against God Jehovah and their propensity to be drawn to idolatry led them through countless cycles of God's discipline. Yet, God's mercy had not been exhausted, nor had His love been extinguished. His love for His creation in general and His people in particular was still the guiding force behind His actions. Although God could easily have justified allowing Haman's plan to move forward in yet another round of chastisement, He chose instead to break through into human history and show unmerited favor.

One of the things we observe in the Old Testament narrative is the importance of God's specific timing. Regardless of our impatience, He is, in fact, never late. And despite our reluctance to move, He is never early. Jane and I used to perform a song entitled "Four Days Late" at our concerts. It was one of my dad's favorites, and he always requested it. The song's message about Lazarus is that even though God seemed to show up four days late, He was right on time!

> But His way is God's way,
>
> not yours or mine
>
> And isn't it great,
>
> when He's four days late He's still on time
>
> Charles Aaron Wilburn & Roberta Wilburn

The key phrase in the book of Esther is, "For such a time as this." Esther found herself in the middle of a dark situation with the future of a nation at stake. She was not there by accident. She was there at the exact time and place to be an integral part of God's plan. She was guided by the hand of God to be the "ordained" solution to the problem. A casual reader could wonder where God is in this story in the first chapter and a half. It seems as though evil would prevail. But as the plot unfolds, it becomes gloriously apparent that, once again, the miracle of God's timing produces precisely the outcome that He desires.

The Tide Can Quickly Change

Have you found yourself in a hopeless, dire circumstance? Perhaps God has plopped you down right in the middle of a particular situation so that you can be an Esther. You are there for such a time as this. It looks like it's going to turn out poorly. But remember that God is a tide-changing God. What looks hopeless to you, already has a God-designed solution. It looked like Haman would win, but he ended up on the hangman's gallows he built for someone else. That's how quickly our God can turn the tables if we are willing, like Esther, to face the opposition and let God work through us courageously.

We tend to believe that everyone else is more capable than we are. We tell ourselves that they are more talented, qualified, and available. We do it to shift the responsibility to someone else and relieve our guilt about not answering the call on our lives. Esther could have done that. No one would have blamed her, and history would have been changed forever without anyone knowing the difference. But she didn't. Instead, she accepted the call to be used by God to save His people from annihilation.

> **Consider this: Not only does God intervene directly in the affairs of humankind with His own hands, but He also places us in specific places at specific times to be His hands. It is then, that we know He has given us a "for such a time as this" assignment.**

God has always opened up doors at the right time. He closes doors at the right time as well.

Michael Chandler

Is there a situation in your life that you feel a particular call or anointing to address?

Perhaps it's a family situation or a conflict at work?

You may have been placed in that situation for "such a time as this." If something doesn't immediately come to mind, ask God to show you why you are where you are right now.

Then, ask Him what your assignment is in that situation. Write down your "sealed orders" when you know what they are.

Don't dismiss them. Each morning, review them and ask God for the strength to carry out your "for such a time as this" assignment.

Snake in the Grass

Snake in the Grass

LOOKING UP FOR HELP

Although we had been warned about snakes and scorpions before the walk, we never saw either. That was a blessing. But there were a multitude of other dangers just as deadly. Vicious wolf-dog hybrids, possible heat stroke, getting lost on the back side of the desert without being able to contact our support vehicle, and walking through a narrow canyon while passing a train that was close enough to reach out and touch: all could have ended the walk in tragedy.

Most of these dangers were what I call "pop-ups." You couldn't plan for them but you always knew they were possible. But we did one simple thing every day, which prevented us from getting into volatile situations more often than we did: We looked at maps. We studied maps for nearly a year before the walk across America started. We ordered specific Route 66 maps, borrowed maps from previous long-distance walkers, and looked at satellite maps, all in an effort to have as few surprises as possible. We got sick of maps. We grew weary of squinting to see the tiny alternate roads we would need to use where Route 66 was gone. We had a love-hate relationship with the maps because some days, they left us with no hope of finding a road and feeling defeated. Other days, they revealed safe passage to the next town down the road.

In one way, maps were dangerous. They could show you that there was no good road ahead. Or they could lead you to believe there was a good road, only to find out the next day that it no longer was there. This sometimes left us in a vulnerable position. But even though there was potential disappointment and danger in what we saw on the map, we had to keep looking at it because it was also our salvation.

This story about Moses and the children of Israel is a similar narrative. The very thing that brought terror and anxiety was the thing that they were asked to look at for salvation: the serpent. Perhaps it's as simple as facing your fears. But maybe it's deeper because, as with so much Scripture, deep and abiding principles are being taught. This one seems particularly hard to grasp because they are being asked to look at the very thing that could kill them. Because, in the end, it will save them.

> 6 The Lord sent fiery serpents among the people and they bit the people, so that many people of Israel died.

7 So the people came to Moses and said, "We have sinned because we have spoken against the Lord and you; intercede with the Lord, that He may remove the serpents from us." And Moses interceded for the people.

8 Then the Lord said to Moses, "Make a fiery serpent, and set it on a standard; and it shall come about, that everyone who is bitten, when he looks at it, he will live."

9 And Moses made a bronze serpent and set it on the standard; and it came about, that if a serpent bit any man when he looked to the bronze serpent, he lived.

Number 21:6-9 NASB95

There are many stories about snakes in the Bible, starting with the Book of Genesis. As a matter of fact, the actor Nicholas Cage once said, "Every great story begins with a snake" (brainyquote.com). The problem with snakes is that you never know if they will save or kill you. Several years ago, we moved to southern Colorado. Snakes were plentiful in the high desert. The first snake I saw there was huge. Later, I found out that it was a bull snake. I was told never to kill a bull snake because they eat rodents like mice and rats. I'm not fond of snakes, but I hate mice and rats, so we let them live. Rattlesnakes were also seen quite often. They are dangerous. They are fast and strike without much warning—those we killed.

We see both kinds of snakes in the story in Numbers 21. Poisonous snakes had invaded the Israelite camp. Their presence reminded Israel of God's intolerance of willful rebellion against His leadership. Their bites were fatal, and terror filled the people of God. Repentance brought the people to their knees and then to Moses for a solution. God's instruction seems almost paradoxical. Moses is told to fashion a bronze snake, put it on a pole, and lift it high. The thing that had bitten them would bring healing when they set their focus on the gold-colored serpent.

This, of course, is another example of God's supernatural intervention in the everyday lives of human beings. He loves to do that, by the way. Just as

He had a miracle for the obstacle of the Jordan River and a provision for the widow's poverty, He had a cure for the curse of the snakes. But one of the things that is so incredible about this story is that the afflicted are asked to look into the face of the very thing that bit them in the first place to be healed. They are instructed to face their fear.

So many times in Scripture, the miraculous answers come through the combination of facing the devil while focusing on God. That is the case in this story. This was also true when Moses faced the Red Sea but focused on the God of Deliverance. Abraham faced the altar where his son was bound and ready to be sacrificed but focused on Jehovah Jireh, the God of Provision. Gideon looked at his puny army, which was outnumbered many times over, but he focused on the God of Victory. Just to remind you, no spiritual armor is provided for the back. You are protected as long as you move toward your enemy in the power of the Lord.

This concept is so counterintuitive and repulsive that we ignore stories like this one. We don't want to face our fears. For most of us, the "fight or flight" instinct is heavily weighted toward flight. Victims don't want to face their attackers because it's just too uncomfortable. I get it. I hate conflict. I'd rather run from my fears than face them any day. But you don't win many victories that way. The challenge is to both face your fear and focus on God. It's a tricky balance to get right. I think that may be one reason God instructed Moses to put the golden serpent on a pole and raise it up. That way, they could see the snake against the backdrop of heaven.

A Snake Handler?

Are you a snake handler? Some people play with snakes, and although I don't encourage that, a part of me admires those who can face their fear so dramatically. Others, maybe most, run from snakes, whether dangerous or not. I recently took my college students on a field trip to Cane Ridge, Kentucky. Some of our young women started screaming as we walked through the grounds. Turns out snakes were crawling through the grass. They were only garter snakes but were the biggest I'd ever seen, probably three feet long. It didn't matter that they were harmless. It only mattered that they were snakes.

We probably scream at many things that aren't really dangerous. But the truth is, we are surrounded by things that are. And we have an adversary who enjoys keeping us bound up in fear. This is why people of faith are asked to wear spiritual bifocals. This enables them to see close-up danger through the near-sighted part of the lens and salvation in the distance through the far-sighted lens. Acknowledging that both danger and deliverance are ahead shows incredible spiritual insight and maturity.

How does this help you live a "supernatural" kind of life? When you learn to live by facing your attacker and focusing on God, you will have the confidence that He is able and willing to come to your rescue whatever happens in your life. Whatever river is raging or shortage is cutting off your supply, He's poised and ready to intervene. Whatever snake has slithered into the camp, do not fear. He is faithful. Walk in that assurance today; before you know it, you may see God's miraculous deliverance.

> **Consider this: For whatever reason, God's solutions sometimes look scary…snake scary. The bridge may wobble. The pill may be difficult to swallow. But remember: There is a good God who is orchestrating it all for our good and His glory (Romans 8:28). Move forward in the assurance that you are more than a conqueror through Christ.**

> You gain strength, courage, and
> confidence by every experience in which
> you really stop to look fear in the face.
>
> Eleanor Roosevelt

What are your greatest fears?

Do you know why you are afraid of them?

List the ones that trouble you or paralyze you the most. Ask God to give you courage in the face of the things which frighten you.

As you are given the opportunity to face them in courage, come back to this list and make note of the victories.

Finishing Strong

Finishing Strong

ENJOYING GOD'S GRACE

One of the most exciting and fulfilling parts of the walk occurred as we walked through America's inner cities. We had purposefully routed ourselves through towns like Albuquerque, Flagstaff, Memphis, Nashville, and the suburbs of Washington, D.C., to have conversations with those living on the streets.

People experiencing homelessness were numerous in the Southwest, where the weather was unseasonably warm as we walked through. As the seasons changed and the temperatures rose as we moved from west to east, we found them to be just as numerous in Amarillo, Oklahoma City, and Knoxville. For the most part, the men and women we met were delightful. We found them polite, respectful, and eager to hear the gospel.

However, a typical response when we shared about Jesus' love was that they felt unworthy. Sometimes, they would begin to recount their many sins and faults. Their wrong choices in the past convinced them that God could not love someone like them. After leading

Anthony to Christ just outside of Los Angeles, we talked to him about where he would spend eternity. He shook his head in disbelief that God could love him that much.

This was not only true for those living on the streets. We found this sentiment in every ethnic group and geographic location regardless of financial success or failure. Most people know they are sinners and can't quite grasp that a holy God would be sympathetic to their plight. But He is!

Christians can feel this way, too. We doubt His ability to use us because of past mistakes, failures, and even outright rebellion toward Him. Indeed, Samson must have felt the same way. He blew it so many times. He turned his back on Yahweh, but God never turned his back on him.

> 28 Then Samson called to the Lord and said, "O Lord God, please remember me and please strengthen me only this once, O God, that I may be avenged on the Philistines for my two eyes."
>
> 29 And Samson grasped the two middle pillars on which the house rested, and he leaned his weight against them, his right hand on the one and his left hand on the other.

30 And Samson said, "Let me die with the Philistines." Then he bowed with all his strength, and the house fell upon the lords and upon all the people who were in it. So, the dead whom he killed at his death were more than those whom he had killed during his life.

Judges 16:28-30

Accounts of those who start strong and finish poorly are common, especially in the Bible. Take Solomon, for example. Following his father's footsteps, he honored God, expanded the kingdom, and built the magnificent temple. Then riches, women, and foreign gods left him a shadow of his former spiritual self. We are left scratching our heads, aren't we? Adam and Eve started well, perfect in fact, and then gave in to temptation and "broke the world" that God had so carefully created. Moses stood firm for so long, struck the rock twice instead of speaking to it, and ended up barred from the Promised Land.

Samson led a life punctuated with the supernatural, lifting city gates, defeating armies with a donkey's jawbone, and breaking free from even the most restrictive restraints. A Nazarite whose strength was woven into his seven locks of hair, Samson became known as Israel's superhero. But his weakness for women led him down the same slippery slope as so many others.

His misplaced affection for Delilah caused him to betray his sacred vow. The Philistines captured him in a weakened state, gouged out his eyes, and enslaved him for use at the grinding mill. What a waste! After such a spiritual and moral failure, it would be expected that God would walk away from Samson and never allow His supernatural power to flow through his body again.

So many men and women have fallen prey to moral impropriety. As I talk with college students and read their papers each semester, I am shocked at how many of them have already compromised themselves in a variety of ways, which causes them to believe that God has written them off. In many cases, their families have cut them off, their churches have shunned them, and sometimes even those who have influenced them to compromise themselves have walked away once they got what they wanted. Is it any wonder they have concluded that God has also turned His back on them? Unfortunately, their expectations have been reinforced by those who are supposed to be their spiritual leaders. They come for spiritual counseling, wanting to know why they can't sense God's presence anymore, and they're told, "Well, how did you expect God to act when you did such a terrible thing?"

Can I be totally honest for a moment? I think there's a little Pharisee in all of us. We kind of want God to withhold His love from people who make a mess of their lives. Everyone except us, that is. We are grateful for His grace toward us, but we want everyone else to pay. Right? This attitude shows through to others and contributes to why those who have failed expect God to abandon them. Did you catch that? They expect God to cut them off.

A God of the Unexpected

But we serve a God who does not always do the expected. Instead of holding a grudge against Samson, He hears his plea for mercy and empowers him to destroy the temple of Dagon. Samson didn't deserve God's favor. Neither do we, which is the point. God does not work through perfect people. Samson was far from perfect. So were Noah, Abraham, and David. He works through willing vessels open enough for God to flow through.

One of the most noteworthy qualities of the Bible is its authenticity. The honesty with which it portrays the characters in its grand narrative is refreshing. By the way, God is all about honesty in our self-evaluation. A pretense of righteousness is neither truthful nor beneficial. Remember the story of the two men who prayed in the temple? One, a Pharisee, thanked God that he was spiritually heads and shoulders above the tax collector. The other, a sinner by all indications, asked for God's mercy because he knew his need for forgiveness. God hears and applauds the sinner who is honest about their spiritual bankruptcy.

This is the meaning of the First Beatitude, "Blessed are the poor in spirit, for theirs is the Kingdom of God" (Matthew 5:3). Jesus is saying that those who realize they are spiritually bankrupt will be blessed. Not because they deserve it but because they acknowledge their inability to attain favor with God on their own. Paul echoes this sentiment by saying, "When I am weak, then I am strong" (II Corinthians 12:10).

The point of Samson's story is that God's mercy is available to all who cry out for it. But not only for redemption. Samson is not just granted forgiveness;

his supernatural strength is restored for one more God-sized miracle. Thank God we are given access to a miraculous life, not because of our perfection, but despite our imperfection.

> **Consider this: If you long for a life where God shows up in extraordinary ways, listen up. You don't have to wait until you've overcome all your shortcomings for God to show up. If ever there was a flawed person, it was Peter. Yet, of all the disciples, he, and he alone, walked on water. He only took a few steps. But aren't a few steps upheld by the supernatural power of God better than none? All the great men and women of God in the Bible and everyone since have been flawed. God used them anyway, and He will use you.**

> I'm not perfect. I'm never going to be. And that's the great thing about living the Christian life and trying to live by faith, is you're trying to get better every day.
>
> Tim Tebow

Answer honestly: Do you feel too flawed to be used by God in miraculous ways?

Is there one thing in your past that causes you to feel that way?

Is it an ongoing habit or sin that you can't seem to get victory over?

No matter what keeps you from believing God wants to use you, it can be forgiven, and you can overcome it with God's help. List those issues here and then write out your request for God to give you an overcoming attitude over your past sins.

An Empty Cradle

An Empty Cradle

BELIEVING EVEN THOUGH

Have you ever made a "deal" with God? I cannot count the number of times I've tried to negotiate an exchange with Him. As a child, I was always what we used to call "husky." It simply meant I was overweight, but most folks were too polite to call me fat. I remember sitting in the bathroom after I'd weighed myself, crying and promising God if He would make me skinny like all my friends, I'd be a missionary. Although it seems a little ridiculous now, there is still a bit of regret that God wasn't willing to sign on to that deal. Please don't misunderstand. He could have done what I asked; He just chose not to. God is a God who can override nature, and although most of the time He decides to let the natural laws that He put into place stand, He can at any moment suspend them.

As we walked across this great nation, we saw God repeatedly hold back the forces of nature. We walked across the mountains near ski resorts, which should have been blanketed with snow, but none had fallen. Tornadoes, which could have quickly taken us out, were held at a safe distance so that we could continue walking. Forecasted storms didn't materialize, severe burns healed much faster than the doctor predicted, and the power of God enabled communication with those who didn't speak English.

There are no easy answers to when God chooses to work this way. I wish I could tell you He will do it anytime you ask. That wouldn't be the truth. And those who preach that message and then chide their hearers who don't experience it for not having enough faith are the worst kind of heretic. The bottom line is that God is sovereign, and His actions are determined by what brings Him glory. There are times when our prayers coincide with His divine will and bring about a suspension of His own rules to accomplish His purpose. By the way, His will always accomplishes what is ultimately best for us and brings Him the highest glory! That's precisely what happened with Hannah. The son she desired was given. That son, Samuel, fulfilled her life's calling and brought God great glory. After all, he was chosen to anoint Israel's first two kings.

> 10 In her deep anguish, Hannah prayed to the Lord, weeping bitterly.
>
> 11 And she made a vow, saying, "Lord Almighty, if you will only look on your servant's misery and remember me, and

not forget your servant but give her a son, then I will give him to the Lord for all the days of his life, and no razor will ever be used on his head."

I Samuel 1:10-11 NIV

The anguish of a woman who desperately wants to have a child and cannot, exceeds the limits of vocabulary. The emptiness and sense of being "less than" can make a woman despair. This was the case with Hannah. Her pain was doubled because her husband's other wife was having children without a problem. Her inexpressible grief was illustrated by Eli's perception that she was "out of her mind" as she prayed. Her despair must have erupted in a flood of imperceptible groans as she prayed. No wonder the priest thought she was drunk!

As a pastor, I have ministered to many women who were childless over the years. Their heart desired to be a mom, but after years of trying and perhaps even spending thousands of dollars on treatment, they had given up hope. Having children is certainly not a necessity. For many women, it is not even a desire. But the emptiness is profound for those who long to sit in the rocking chair with a child in their arms. This was Hannah's story.

Her predicament can produce a sense of empathy in anyone who has faced the challenges of the laws of nature. Her barrenness was not curable by human means. This was just the way it was. When we face an impossible medical diagnosis or the addiction of a loved one, we are tempted to feel hopeless, knowing we are fighting the forces of nature that the Creator put in place.

As products of The Enlightenment and the Modern Age, most of us are convinced that science and the laws of nature trump everything else. The law of gravity dictates that things fall down, not up. The position of the earth and sun determines the length of a day and the change of seasons. Heavy objects do not float on top of the water. We accept these facts without question, and most of us never ask God to violate the principles He designed. It seems futile since He affirmed these principles by calling them "good."

A God Who Can Overrule Nature

But wait. That's the key, isn't it? He is the Creator who established those parameters, and since He is an omnipotent God, He can suspend them whenever He chooses. God, at creation, instituted those laws with good reason, but nothing precludes Him from temporarily turning things upside down to satisfy His will and purpose. As a matter of fact, the examples above show that God can temporarily suspend these rules of the universe whenever He pleases. Instead of the Jordan River flowing downstream, it is raised "up" in a heap (Joshua 3). The sun stood still to give victory to Joshua (Joshua 10), and an axe head, which should have sunk, floated on top of the water (II Kings 6).

Many more of the miracles in the Old Testament involve nature being overruled by God. He prevents a fiery furnace from burning the three Hebrew children. He raises a child from the dead. He causes a donkey to speak. And, although God generally works within His guidelines, He is free to color "outside the lines" whenever He chooses. One of God's names is Jehovah Sabaoth (יהוה צבאות), which means the Lord of Hosts. He is Lord over all the universe and all of its powers.

> "When you pray to Jehovah Sabaoth, you are praying to a God so magnificent that all creation serves His purposes."
>
> **Ann Spangler**

And that is precisely what He does with Hannah. A previously childless woman becomes a mother to one of the heroes of our faith, Samuel. A woman who is physically unable to have a child delivers a healthy baby boy. The lesson? Not only is nothing too difficult for God, but there is no natural law or limitation He cannot override to supply what we need and what will ultimately give Him the glory.

I am always saddened by those who have chosen to believe that God has either lost the ability or His desire to do the miraculous. I can't find anything in Scripture to support that belief. I know people have different opinions about whether or not specific "sign gifts" are still valid, and I think there's room for loving disagreement on those issues. But hopefully, that's not an argument about God's ability to do certain things. God has not changed, either in His abilities or His purpose. When He sovereignly chooses to part waters, I believe he still can. When He chooses to defy gravity or open blind eyes, He can. He is still God and still sits on His throne!

> Consider this: If you are childless, penniless, hopeless, or homeless, there is nothing that God cannot do. He can make things fall up instead of down. He can take a terminal diagnosis and change it into a favorable prognosis. He's God! Nothing is too hard for Him. Don't limit your prayers to what can be understood or explained. Pray big prayers!

The God who made the rules that govern the universe also has the authority to set them aside. And on occasion, He has, if it was necessary, to serve His purposes.

Billy Graham

What force of nature is standing in the way of your breakthrough?

Is there a medical issue, a physical limitation, or some natural phenomenon that has caused you to lose hope?

Write a letter to God explaining how this affects your life and your ability to live victoriously. Ask Him if he plans to change the situation or to help you get through it. Commit in advance to abide in faith, regardless of His plan.

Muddy Water

Muddy Water

Obeying God's Instructions

Are You Kidding Me, God?

When you are trying to do the right thing and follow God's will, it kind of stinks when things go wrong. I think many of us live under the impression that when we're trying to be obedient, God will hold back the attacks on us and give us a smooth path. To say that concept is a faulty one is a significant understatement.

I suppose when we started walking across America, we knew there would be hard days and physical pain. But we could never have imagined what we were going to experience. There were blisters, sun poisoning, allergic reactions, falls, bad weather, and 2nd and 3rd-degree burns that sent me to the Burn Center in Little Rock, Arkansas.

But I think for me, one of the worst weeks occurred as we were walking through Nashville. We had had a last-minute replacement for our support vehicle driver. We had to get an axle replaced. While replacing it, they crushed the oil pan. We had to rent a pick-up truck which had none of our supplies in it. It rained off and on all week. I experienced a severe allergic reaction and couldn't breathe. And then, the icing on the cake, I got a horrible stomach bug. I remember thinking, "God, here I am, doing what you asked me to do, and all of this in one week? Are you kidding me, God?"

I know it sounds awful, but I felt pretty beat up. I never felt that walking across America was beneath us. We weren't famous or well-known. We had no delusions of grandeur. But, at this point, I was beginning to feel as though what God was asking was a little much (just being honest here). I bet you've felt that way at least a few times in your life, right? Sometimes, it seems that the harder we try and the more faithful we are, the worse things get. I wonder if the Apostle Paul ever felt that way. It seems like the more determined he was to take the gospel to the world, the more he suffered: Shipwrecks, beatings, snake bites, stoning, and imprisonment.

Perhaps that's how Naaman felt. Already feeling embarrassed and experiencing social shunning because of his leprosy, he now has to humble himself even more. He went to see the great prophet, Elisha, hoping for a miracle. Naaman probably thought Elisha would wave a magic wand over his body, and he'd be healed. Or maybe recite an incantation or give him a prescription, and all would be well. When he got the instructions, he must have thought, "God, are you kidding me?"

> 10 Elisha sent out a servant to meet him with this message: "Go to the River Jordan and immerse yourself seven times. Your skin will be healed, and you'll be as good as new."

> 14 So he did it. He went down and immersed himself in the Jordan seven times, following the orders of the Holy Man. His skin was healed; it was like the skin of a little baby. He was as good as new.

>> II Kings 5:10, 14 (The Message)

Sometimes, the way to deliverance humbles us. God's answer is sometimes embarrassing, seemingly beneath us, or even humiliating. Perhaps that's how Naaman felt. Surely, there were more respectable ways to be healed. Weren't there cleaner rivers than the Jordan? And by the way, couldn't the prophet himself have made an appearance? We can't be sure why Elisha sent these particular instructions to Naaman, but one thing is for sure: Naaman had to eat a great big piece of humble pie that day.

Those in positions of power often struggle with having high opinions of themselves and their capabilities. Intellectuals struggle to not depend on their own "smarts" to solve their problems. Millionaires and billionaires sitting inside their palatial mansions believe their wealth will overcome all their challenges. No matter what they possess, the "haves" always struggle with simple obedience that does not depend on their resources or status to solve the issue.

However, humility is a prominent theme throughout scripture. God promises to heal our land when we humble ourselves (II Chron. 7:14). He resists the proud but gives grace to the humble (I Peter 5:5). And finally, for God to lift us, we must be humble (James 4:10). Many times, God's inability or perhaps it's more accurate to say, His unwillingness to supernaturally intervene in our lives boils down to a problem with pride.

Pride deceives us into believing that we don't need God. Maybe we have a Ph.D., a fancy title, a big bank account, or lots of trophies on the mantle. We expect God to work within our parameters. We want miracles that don't tarnish our image or dirty our clothes. And for goodness sake, don't mess up our perfectly quaffed hairdo!

Putting a list of conditions on God doesn't alter His work...it stops it! He refuses to get into our ideological or theological boxes. He doesn't negotiate the terms of His activity in our lives. He's God, and He's allowed to call the shots. It really is His way or the highway; generally speaking, His highway doesn't arrive at our desired location. This is why we often miss out on the miraculous lifestyle God would love for us to enjoy. This doesn't mean that every occurrence in our lives will be "walking on water" miraculous. But it does mean that we will walk through this life with the certainty that whatever God asks us to do, wherever He leads us to go, will be a lifelong journey where seeing the supernatural intervention of God in our lives will be a fairly common occurrence.

Naaman had a decision to make: He could stay proud and sick or humble himself and be healed. It may have been reluctantly at first, but with each of the seven dips in the river, he became aware that his heart was being changed along with his leprous skin. The key to his miracle was not the muddy water. It was in his being humble enough to submit to the will and purpose of God. That's our key, too.

Like Naaman, we, too, must make a decision. We can stay proud and be resisted by the God who would rather embrace us. Or we can humble ourselves and be surrounded by His presence. We can count on our initiatives and abilities and ultimately be disappointed. Or we can admit our inability to fix ourselves and our problems and see God work as only He can. We can allow our egos to swell and our spirits to shrink, or let our heads return to their normal size, and see our spirits soar. The decision is up to us.

> **Consider this: A healthy self-image is beneficial. Knowing who you are in Christ is a real blessing. But an arrogant self-image is dangerous. Paul advised that when we think we are standing in our power, we should take heed because we are about to trip and fall. Remember: A person stands tallest when they are on their knees.**

> Knowledge is proud that it knows so much; wisdom is humble that it knows no more.
>
> William Cowper

Is God asking you to do something that you feel is beneath you?

Write it down. Is there something you feel called to do that isn't what you want to do?

Write it down. Has God put a desire in your heart to serve others, but there are people around you who think you're "better than that?"

Write it down. Take what you've written down and compare it to what Jesus did when He washed the disciples' feet. Pray and ask God for the willingness to serve, to be last and not first, or even to be embarrassed if it will lift up Jesus.

God Always Has A Bear

God Has a Bear

Knowing God's Got It

My youngest sister, Susan, came to drive our support vehicle for us in Virginia. She did a great job and greatly encouraged us as we finished the last few hundred miles of the walk across America. We were barely able to walk by this time in our journey. As we got ready to begin each day, my sister would yell out her daily mantra. Susan, who passed away in December 2022, had a favorite saying. She said it all the time, and honestly, there were times when I wondered if she really believed it. I was afraid that it had just become one of those things that people say without thinking much about what it means. During her last few months, I discovered that she really lived by this adage: "God's got this!"

Susan seemed to have more than her share of medical/physical challenges in her life. She battled a lot of the same hereditary issues that our family has dealt with over the years. Routine surgeries always seemed to become anything but routine for Susan. In addition, her daughters went through some rough patches, which always caused her great concern. When our parents got sick, Susan took it the hardest, and I'm not sure she ever wholly recovered from their passing.

But you know what? You seldom saw Susan without a smile. She was an encourager. As an elementary school teacher, she was loved by her students and co-workers alike. Practically, the entire school staff showed up for her memorial service. The teachers talked about how she would send positive, encouraging texts to them every day to brighten their mornings. She invested her life in others and reminded them often when they were going through difficult times that "God's got this!"

This is the attitude that faith fosters. This is the evidence of "things not seen." Susan could not see what was on the other side of her trials, but she believed in a God who had it all under control. I said she couldn't see the other side, but there was one exception. Not long before Susan passed, she had another "routine" surgery. There were several errors made during and immediately following the surgery that put her in a coma, and she almost died. She recovered temporarily, and Jane and I went to visit her in the hospital. While we were there, she explained something that happened while unconscious. She looked at us and said, "I saw Jesus." She teared up a little and repeated, "I saw Jesus."

She was explaining, "I know what's ahead, but I've seen the other side." All of her adult life, she had been telling others that even though they couldn't see how

God would work it out, they could rest assured that He would. Now, it seemed like God was rewarding her by personally showing up to say, "I've got this, Susan. It's going to be OK." The Bible is full of "God's got this" stories. This one is one of my favorites.

> 23 Then he went up from there to Bethel; and as he was going up by the way, young boys came out from the city and mocked him and said to him, "Go up, you baldhead; go up, you baldhead!"
>
> 24 Then he looked behind him and saw them. And he cursed them in the name of Yahweh. Then, two female bears came out of the woods and tore up forty-two lads of their number.
>
> 25 And he went from there to Mount Carmel, and from there he returned to Samaria.
>
> II Kings 2:23-25 Legacy Standard Bible

The second chapter of Second Kings begins and ends with the miraculous. Actually, there are miracles in the middle, too! At the beginning of the chapter, Elijah is taken away in a chariot of fire. His protege, Elisha, is bold enough to follow Elijah persistently, even when asked to stay behind. Finally, just before being carried away, Elijah asked Elisha what he desired. He asked for a double portion of the spirit of Elijah!

What an insightful request. He could have asked for anything. He could have petitioned his mentor for fame and notoriety as a prophet. He could have sought great fortune or a beautiful wife. What would you have asked for? Would your "ask" have been as spiritually mature? I am ashamed to admit it, but most of my "gimme" prayers are for things much less impactful than a double portion of Godly power and vision.

When Elijah's mantle falls on his student, a double portion also falls on him. Immediately, the power of God begins to work through him. For example, The unsafe water was transformed by simply adding a jar full of salt. Now, the water was healthy and could support life. The miracle-working power of God was obviously present in Elisha's life and ministry. One of the attributes of God's presence in our lives is the evidence that proves He is with us. Elisha immediately began to see the evidence of God's supernatural power.

> I see the evidence of Your goodness
>
> All over my life, all over my life
>
> I see Your promises in fulfillment
>
> All over my life, all over my life
>
> Cash, Hulse, and Baldwin

How would it change your attitude if you felt you had a double portion of God's power and blessing on your walk through life today? Would your steps be a little quicker knowing you were walking covered by the mantle of Elijah? Would it prompt you to stop and minister to those in need? Would you give more freely of your resources if you were convinced God would give back, shaken together and running over?

This must have been Elisha's attitude. He was walking on air. Maybe he was humming a tune. Maybe now and then, he skipped. However he celebrated, the party must have ended rather abruptly. On Elisha's way back to Bethel, he is confronted by young hooligans who poke fun at the new prophet's lack of hair. This was more serious than simple teasing. It must have been an attack on his calling as God's spokesperson, or perhaps even blasphemy against God. Whatever it was, it prompted Elisha to proclaim a "curse." Immediately, God sends two she-bears to eliminate the hecklers. What an unfortunate way to go!

What's the Point?

Miracles happen in all kinds of situations. Sometimes, perhaps most of the time, they provide or supply something. God gave manna in the wilderness, water in the desert, fire on Mount Carmel, and rain to end a drought. However, one of the most neglected types of miracles is the supernatural elimination of something that needs to go. These delinquents needed to go. Elisha didn't deal with them; he left them to an all-powerful God. We often get into trouble by trying to eliminate our own problematic situations. But God can make things disappear as quickly as He can make them appear. The key is not to stress over your enemies or unwanted opposition: God always has a bear!

> Consider this: God has a miraculous way of providing what we need and also eliminating what we don't need. What seems like a "takeaway" may be God making room for His next blessing. Someone wiser than me once said: Sometimes, the quickest route to addition is through subtraction. Pray for both kinds of miracles: Addition and subtraction. Sometimes, God wants to take away what you don't need so He can bless you with what you do need. Don't sweat those who make fun, belittle, and cast aspersions. God always has a bear! God's got this!

"Never avenge yourselves, but leave it to the wrath of God, for it is written, 'Vengeance is mine, I will repay,' says the Lord."

The Apostle Paul to the Romans

Is there a thorn in your flesh that you'd like to remove?

It's tempting to try to take care of the problem ourselves. But when we do, we sometimes cause more damage than good.

Think of three things in your life that are discouraging your spiritual progress. The first could be a person. The second might be a habit. The third could be a grudge or unforgiveness toward someone.

Write a prayer asking God to either remove the spiritual obstacle or direct you toward victory over, under, around, or through it to get to the other side.

A Fish Story

A Fish Story

REPENTING AFTER A FALL

By the time God called us to walk across America, we had learned the hard way (several times) that it's best to yield to His will rather than run in the opposite direction. Most people have to learn through experience that submitting to God's purpose for their lives is a much better way to live. I wish I had discovered it sooner.

I spent all of my life in ministry. I sang for the first time in church when I was three. I started playing the piano and then the organ a few years later at about 9 or 10 years old. I started preaching at 14 and have filled some sort of church staff position or traveled in full-time evangelism for most of the rest of my life. There are, however, a couple of exceptions.

When we began to write this book, I decided we would be as honest and transparent as possible. We're not perfect, and we never want to give that impression. Although we talk about many victories and ways that God has come through for us (and He has), there have been times when we failed to be faithful to Him. We're hoping that as we share those times, too, you'll be encouraged that God can use you, regardless of your spiritual resume.

1984 was challenging for our family. The church I was pastoring closed its doors due to some broken promises of support. As a result, some members surmised that it was because of the mishandling of funds. That was not the case, and I did not personally handle any of the money. Nothing ever became of the accusations; however, the local newspaper, which had supported our church and covered several of our events, got wind of the allegations and called wanting an interview. I had a wife and three small children. I was pastoring in the community where my father had pastored for many years and where I had graduated from high school. All I could think of was the shame that the publicity would cause my family and parents to go through. Although I knew I was innocent, I wasn't sure I could handle the pressure of dealing with such a huge and potentially damaging situation.

I was 28 years old and imagined that this could be the end of my ministry. Although I hate to admit it, I thought it might also be the end of my life. I contemplated whether or not my family would be better off without me. I got in the old car we were driving and knew if I drove it off a bridge, it would be easily mistaken for a car malfunction and an accidental death. To this day,

I'm not sure who was praying for me, but someone was whispering my name to Jesus and He to the Father. I couldn't go through with it. I turned around and went home to my family.

This is the backstory of our move to Denver. After all of this, I wanted out. I was burned out on church and church people. I wanted to get as far away from those who had caused this pain as possible. Although I wasn't particularly mad at God, He became the scapegoat for my anger. I didn't want to preach. I never wanted to be that vulnerable again. And so I ran. We ran. We ran all the way across the country to Denver to avoid the call on our lives. We didn't end up in the belly of a great fish, but we were pretty miserable. A year later, we moved back home and had, in that time, learned a very valuable lesson: It's never wise to run from God's call. So when God spoke to us some 20 years later about walking across America, we didn't balk. We said yes.

> 17 And the Lord appointed a great fish to swallow up Jonah. And Jonah was in the belly of the fish for three days and three nights.
>
> Jonah 1:17 ESV

The story of Jonah is one of the most ridiculed in the Old Testament. Skeptics have always pointed out the difficulties in believing a human could be swallowed whole by a fish, remain there for three days, survive, and then be spit out on dry land in good condition. Even as I type this story, it seems far-fetched.

As a child growing up in Western New York, there was an amusement park that our family frequented. The park, Fantasy Island, included depictions of fanciful, make-believe stories that entertained children in addition to food and rides. One of the popular displays was of a giant whale. You could walk up a ramp and look down into the belly of the whale through a gigantic open mouth. Deep inside the fish, an animated Jonah sat at a table, eating a meal and waving at the children as they walked by. The message was clear. This fairy tale had no basis in reality and was as real as Cinderella, Popeye, and Old Mother Hubbard.

There are, however, many reasons to believe the story's authenticity, not the least of which is that Jesus believed it. There is even anecdotal evidence. Several verifiable accounts of people surviving such ordeals have now been documented. But the integrity of the story is not the point here. Instead, let's consider the far-reaching implications of this miracle in the believer's life.

First, Jonah comes dangerously close to missing the real miracle. Literally, the real miracle, the one that God had planned all along, was the revival in Nineveh. But that's the very miracle that Jonah actually wanted to avoid. Nineveh, the capital of Assyria (Israel's enemy), was the last place on earth where Jonah wanted to be a missionary. It was also the last place he wanted to see God extend His mercy. And so he ran in the opposite direction.

God wanted Jonah to be the catalyst for renewal. God always uses people to proclaim His Word. He confirms that in the New Testament with Paul's letter to the church at Rome.

> 14 How then will they call on him in whom they have not believed? And how are they to believe in him of whom they have never heard? And how are they to hear without someone preaching?
>
> Romans 10:14 ESV

The reluctant preacher, Jonah, wanted so badly to avoid being a part of the spiritual awakening that he boarded a ship that would have taken him 2500 miles away. Encouraging him to answer the call wouldn't be easy, but God performed several other miracles to facilitate the repentance of Jonah and then Nineveh. First, God created a storm so ferocious that it terrified seasoned sailors. Second, He caused the lots to fall on Jonah, indicating that Jonah was the reason for the storm. Third, He prepared a great fish capable of swallowing a human whole. Fourth, He kept Jonah alive and had the fish spit him up on the shore. Notice God's persistent effort to get Jonah back to the original plan. God doesn't give up. God pursues those He desires to use. He's got your number, and he's going to keep calling until you answer.

Please hear this truth: You are never so far off the path that God cannot miraculously work situations and circumstances to get you back on track. He didn't write you off somewhere along the way. He is patient and is constantly rerouting your life to get you back to His original destination (plan). Like a car's GPS, it will only stop rerouting once you return to the correct route. Your GPS will never say, "I'm sorry, you've made too many wrong turns, so I'm giving up on you." Neither will God!

> **Consider this: God is committed to having you on the path that will honor Him and be best for you. He promises that in Romans 8:28. Wherever you are, regardless of how badly you've messed up, relax. Submit to God, ask for His guidance, and follow His direction.**

"It's important to understand that at every point of opposition to who we are or to what God has called us to do, we are presented with the options of either conforming and giving in, or standing our ground and becoming stronger in who God has made us to be."

Gabriel Wilson-Ancient Faith Ministries

Have you ever run away from God's calling?

Has there ever been a time when you told God no?

Maybe you weren't quite that bold, so you delayed your answer, hoping God would move on to someone else. If so, has there ever been a time when you repented of that action and, one, asked for forgiveness, and two, told God you would do what He asked?

If not, why not write a few sentences about where you are in that process and ask God to help you have a willing heart?

Tunnel Vision

Tunnel Vision

Digging Down Deep

One of the questions we are often asked when we talk about our cross-country walk is whether or not we were walkers or hikers before the walk. The answer is always a resounding "No!" Neither of us were athletic...at all. This is one of the things that make the walk even more miraculous. God asked two middle-aged people with no long-distance walking experience to take off and walk nearly 3000 miles from coast to coast in six months!

Please listen very carefully. We give God 100% of the credit for completing our journey. We know He sustained us and carried us from one side of the country to the other. However, we also know that had we not prepared and trained, we would never have lasted. The year before the walk, we started walking. At first, just a mile or two a day. Then more. Eventually, after several months, we could walk ten miles. The year before the walk across America, we walked 1500 miles. We went on a diet and lost weight. We read everything we could find about shoes, socks, rain gear, and Route 66. In other words, we worked while we waited for God's provision.

This is where a lot of people need clarification. God does "have it". He will empower you to do whatever He has called you to do. It is His mission, not yours, and He will complete it. But, as my kids used to say, "God gave you two good legs." In other words, God will not roll you across the country in a wheelchair if you've got two good legs. He won't take the test for you just because you didn't study and use the brain He put in your head. God expects you to prepare, work, and do what you can as a seed of faith. He will always honor that seed by making it grow. But generally speaking, He's not going to plant it for you. That's on you.

There's a fine line between dependence upon God and laziness. Waiting on God is not necessarily the same as sitting on the couch. You'll notice that in my favorite verse (Isaiah 40:31), it says that those who wait will "walk" and "run." Waiting and depending on God is accompanied by activity. As a matter of fact, it is our activity that shows our faith. This is why James says, "Faith without works is dead." Faith is an action word. We don't really "have" faith in God…we "do" faith in God.

This is an analogy that may help. Dynamite is detonated by a much smaller explosion caused by something called a blasting cap. If you watch the planned demolition of a building using dynamite, you'll see tiny explosions that happen first. They produce a little puff of smoke. Then, a much larger explosion occurs bringing the building down in a massive cloud of dust. The blasting cap ignites the sticks of dynamite, and that's where the real power lies. Interestingly, the Greek word for power is "dunimis," which is where we get our word dynamite.

The blasting cap is your action, planning, training, studying, and sowing seed. God's supernatural power is the dynamite. It takes both. Your work is the trigger that blasts away the obstacles.

> The rest of the events of Hezekiah's reign, along with all his might and how he made the pool and the tunnel and brought water into the city, are written in the Historical Record of Judah's Kings.
>
> II Kings 20:20 CSB

The story of King Hezekiah is one of my favorites in the Old Testament. Part of its attraction for me is that so many people don't know the story, or at least not the details. Typical Sunday School stories get discussed a lot. The history surrounding Hezekiah and his tunnel is, for some reason, ignored for the most part. When I teach university students about this miraculous event, I love watching them put everything else aside and start listening intently.

Hezekiah was among the few good kings who ruled the Southern Kingdom of Judah. The Northern Kingdom of Israel had already fallen to Assyria, and so had many of the strongholds in Judah. Jerusalem was the crown jewel of Judah, and Sennacherib was determined to conquer it. As a matter of fact, as he laid siege on the city, he arrogantly boasted about his ability to starve the inhabitants out and plunder the city.

One of the ways Sennacherib planned to sustain the siege and force surrender by the inhabitants of Jerusalem was to secure the only water supply for himself and his soldiers. But God had already given Hezekiah a plan. A tunnel was dug through solid stone, 1750 feet long, which diverted the water supply into and through the city and kept it from being accessible to Sennacherib's army.

Now, here is the miracle. The men who dug the tunnel started at two opposite ends. They picked their way through solid stone without the benefit of modern technology and met precisely in the middle. Not only did the two ends line up, but the slope of the tunnel floor was just the right decline to keep water flowing from one end to the other. The grade of the tunnel also matched perfectly when the two teams merged!

Can you imagine being in a dark tunnel, picking your way through solid rock, having no real sense of where you are, and hoping you will meet the other group of laborers in the middle? It would have seemed hopeless and futile. But one day, as they were digging, they heard the sound of metal against stone in the distance. What excitement must have filled their hearts? They may have even shrugged their shoulders and thought, "How in the world did we do that?"

Of course, we know in retrospect that they didn't. God did. But the story of Hezekiah's Tunnel has a tremendous lesson for us to learn. While Hezekiah was trusting God for victory, he was not idle. Faith does not equal inactivity. It's actually quite the opposite. Faith is not something we possess nearly as much as it is something we do. While waiting and believing, they were also digging! There is no such thing as idle faith.

> Yet those who wait for the LORD Will gain new strength; They will mount up with wings like eagles, They will run and not get tired, They will walk and not become weary.
>
> Isaiah 40:31 NASB95

The above verse is my (Rick) life verse. It has been significant to my wife and me over the years. But I wonder if we fail to grasp the profound truth within this passage. We tend to be motivated to "wait," yet we are not nearly as eager to fly, run, and walk long distances. Could it be that the strength comes when we fly as we wait? I believe the key is that you must run to "not get tired" and walk to "not become weary." This changes everything, doesn't it?

So Hezekiah works while he waits. It seems counterintuitive. But remember, he doesn't say, "Those who rest," he says, "those who wait." The miracle of the tunnel happened when they labored in obedience to God. The walls of Jericho fell when they walked. Naaman's leprosy vanished as he dipped repeatedly in the Jordan River. Your miracle will likely come in the same way.

The miracle of the tunnel is followed up by another where a warrior angel of the Lord blindsides Sennacherib's army. They return to Nineveh in defeat, and God's miracle-working power is again demonstrated on behalf of His people.

> **Consider this: If you are praying for a miracle, trusting God for the impossible, work while you wait. Get up and run toward the goal. Press on, keep walking. The impossible rarely comes with idleness.**

"I am not waiting for a move of God; I am a move of God."

William Booth Founder of
the Salvation Army

What can you do while you wait for your miracle?

Without trying to do God's work, is there something you can do that needs to be done?

Can you use your ability or talent to remove roadblocks and clear the way for the miracle to arrive?

Write them down and then check them off when you complete them.

Saved By Thorns

Saved By Thorns

TRUSTING HIS PROVISION

A promise doesn't mean what it used to mean. My father used to talk about a time when a person's word was his bond. Houses, land, horses, and farm equipment were bought and sold with a promise to provide and a promise to pay. A laborer went to work by shaking hands with the boss. One promised to pay, the other to work. Marriages were less likely to end in divorce 200 years ago, at least partly due to the seriousness with which the couple made their promises to each other. Unfortunately, a twenty-first-century promise must be considered simply a good intention rather than a sacred vow. It's as likely to be broken as it is to be kept.

The Bible is full of promises. But not everything in the Bible is a promise; some folks get into trouble with that theology. Some of what we read in Scripture are general principles and precepts. They are guidelines for living that teach us that if we do or don't do certain things, we can generally expect a specific outcome. Proverbs is an excellent example of this.

However, we can count on the hundreds of promises that God does make. For example, Jesus said that He would always be with us and that He would never leave us or forsake us. That's a promise. You can bank on it. God promised never to destroy the earth again with a global flood. That's a promise, and He even sealed the promise with a sign in the sky: the rainbow. Paul asserted that God would supply our needs according to His riches in heaven. That's a promise, and it should bring comfort to your heart.

The problem with human promises is that flawed human beings make them. Even with the best of intentions, we sometimes fail to keep our word. The beautiful thing about God's promises is that he cannot be unfaithful to His word. He cannot lie. So when you are sure it is a promise from God to you*, you can believe it and stand upon the truth of it.

Trust God. Trust the story He has written for your life. Trust that He will supply everything you need to accomplish everything He has called you to do. Wait on His provision and the fulfillment of His promise. His supply is more plenteous, better quality, and more blessed than anything you could ever provide for yourself. He is Jehovah-Jireh, the God who provides.

*All promises in the Bible are not universal. Some are promises made to people or nations for specific times. Please always look at the context of the promise to see if this is a promise you can legitimately claim.

> 13 Then Abraham raised his eyes and looked, and behold, behind him a ram caught in the thicket by his horns; and Abraham went and took the ram and offered him up for a burnt offering in the place of his son.
>
> 14 Abraham called the name of that place The Lord Will Provide, as it is said to this day, "In the mount of the Lord it will be provided."
>
> Genesis 22: 13-14 NASB95

The story of Abraham and Isaac on Mount Moriah is one of the hardest in the Old Testament for me to read. Being the father of one son makes this an emotionally charged narrative. Each time I read it or teach it to my Old Testament college students, I cannot comprehend the angst and uncertainty that must have filled the heart and mind of Abraham.

The miracle of this story begins long before Abraham and Isaac make their three-day trek up the mountain. Abraham was to be the Father of many nations, yet he had no children. But God had promised. Although Abraham and Sarah were well beyond the age of siring and birthing a child, God promised a son, and Isaac was born. And now, the son of promise, the one through whom the covenant would be fulfilled, was to be sacrificed. None of it made sense. Humanly speaking, it seemed like a very cruel trick. But God had promised.

Of course, Abraham could not possibly have understood that as this whole event unfolded, it was an incredibly accurate foreshadowing of the Messiah to come. The three-day journey, the sacrificing of the only son, the one to be sacrificed carrying the wood, and both having their hands bound all pointed to the story's apex. God would send a ram to serve as a substitute sacrifice for Isaac. A perfect lamb, caught in a thicket, a "crown of thorns," would die in place of a flawed man (Isaac). Two thousand years later, a Perfect Lamb, caught in a crown of thorns, would die in place of a flawed human race. The redemption cycle would be completed on a mountain, most likely visible to Abraham as he held the knife in his outstretched hand:

Mount Calvary.

What seems miraculous to us is simply God fulfilling His promises. It's extraordinary for us because faithfulness and promise-keeping are rare commodities in our culture. I have found myself doubting practically everything I read on the Internet or hear on newscasts because people have no hesitation about being dishonest. People don't keep appointments. They don't meet their obligations. They are unfaithful to their spouses. What's the point? We aren't used to people doing what they say, and when they do, we're shocked. We don't depend on people because they're not dependable. God is just the opposite, but we forget that sometimes.

Part of living the victorious life God desires for us is simply counting on God. Believe that He will do what He said He will do. He promised Abraham a son, and He kept His promise. He promised him descendants, and He kept His word. The Bible is packed with promises from a good and loving Father. Believe that He will keep His commitment. God promised His followers "mountain-moving" power. Believe it. He promised to supply all of your needs. Believe it! Jesus promised that those who believe in Him will never die. Believe it.

When He comes through, it will seem supernatural, but that's from our perspective. From where God sits,

He's just acting naturally. He's just being Himself. This is one crucial reason why we must pray that God would give us the mind of Christ (Phil. 2:5). Christ saw blind people seeing, lame people walking, deaf people hearing, dead people living, and a boy's small lunch feeding five thousand. Why? Because He understood that His Father's desire, ability, and faithfulness intersected in a place called "faith." This kind of faith, based on knowing what God wants, what He can do, and that He will do what He promised, produces ageless faith, the kind that stands the test of time.

This is where God wants us to live: On the cutting edge of faith. To see what He sees, to feel what He feels, and to respond as He responds. This is real life. This is victorious living. This is living supernaturally instead of naturally. This should be our baseline for living. Any other kind of living is just existing. It's subnormal.

> As Christians, we have lived a subnormal life for so long that when we finally begin to live the normal Christian life, people call us abnormal.
>
> Jack Taylor

> **Consider this: What God promised...He will accomplish. He will do it in His time and His way, but He will keep His Word. Victorious living happens when we know God's promises and behave like we believe He will keep them. Read His Word, memorize His promises, and step out in faith.**

"The best-praying man is the man who is most believingly familiar with the promises of God. After all, prayer is nothing but taking God's promises to him, and saying to him, "Do as thou hast said." Prayer is the promise utilized. A prayer which is not based on a promise has no true foundation."

Charles Spurgeon

List five promises that are especially relevant to your life right now.

Keep the list handy during your prayer time each day. Remind God of His promises, and ask Him to apply His promises to your situations.

Do this until the answer comes. When it does, return to your list and record the answer to your prayer.

A Salt-Free Diet

A Salt-Free Diet

Resisting Temptation

Most of us don't like to disclose our temptations. We don't want to be judged by others or embarrassed by our weakness in a particular area. You've probably heard the adage, "Confession is good for the soul," but most of us see it as beneficial only with some limitations.

Besides, admitting to temptation, especially if we confess yielding to its allure, tarnishes our halo. And we love to keep up our pious reputation. The reluctance to be honest about temptation is especially strong in those who are our spiritual leaders. We want pastors who are above temptation and live in constant victory over sin.

When Jane and I share about the walk across America, we talk about the victories. There were hundreds of "wins" along the way where we saw God come through miraculously. But most of those mountaintop experiences came after wrestling with temptation in the valley.

For example, one of the most challenging aspects of the walk was dealing with some of our drivers who came to drive our support vehicle each day. Before I go on, let me say this: Most of our drivers were excellent, and we could not have finished the walk without everyone who came to help. But, a few were sure they had a better, more efficient method or were directionally challenged. Walking twenty-plus miles each day was grueling. We were tired, sore, hurting, missing our families, and burnt out for much of the walk. We needed encouragement, smiles, great attitudes, and lots of love. Most gave us that and much more, but the ones who were out of sorts, grumpy, critical, and couldn't find their way tempted us to lose our religion more than once. Honestly, I wanted to lose more than my religion. I wanted to lose a driver... permanently, a few times.

God was good; we usually resisted the temptation to lose our cool. And it seemed like great ones always followed the problematic drivers. But the temptation was always there to look back, to dwell on the mistakes and attitudes of the difficult weeks, rather than praise God for the good ones. Part of it was human nature and the stress of the walk, but neither was a legitimate excuse. The lesson was driven home, mile after mile: Look forward, not back.

There is a story in the Old Testament about someone

who looked back. She longed for the sinful lifestyle she had enjoyed in the wicked city of Sodom. She was warned not to look, but she did and paid a horrible price.

> The sun had risen over the earth when Lot came to Zoar. Then the LORD rained on Sodom and Gomorrah brimstone and fire from the LORD out of heaven, and He overthrew those cities, and all the valley, and all the inhabitants of the cities, and what grew on the ground. But his wife, from behind him, looked back, and she became a pillar of salt.
>
> Genesis 19: 23-26 NASB95

Sodom was a wicked city. It was so wicked, in fact, that it earned a unique kind of God's wrath: Fire and brimstone. Without going into detail, the debauchery that permeated this city was the raunchy, perverted kind that turns God's stomach. Had it not been for Abraham's intervention on Lot's behalf, it is very possible that he, too, would have been destroyed. Don't misunderstand; Lot was no saint. He allowed his family to live in the closest thing to hell on earth that we can imagine. His children were raised in evil's presence with apparently no plans to remedy the situation. Lot did, however, redeem himself enough to be spared by protecting the angels sent by God from being raped by the sexually perverted men of the city.

As the angels led Lot and his family to safety, they were instructed not to look back. The city was being bombarded with what must have looked like flaming meteorites. The cries of agony as those inside burned alive could be heard well outside the city walls. The children must have been terrified, and the warning to look ahead rather than back would have spared them many future nightmares. That warning can be applied to our lives as well. Looking back at past tragedies, moral failures, and seasons of emotional trauma generally leads to reliving those experiences through negative memories and frightening dreams. Both of these feed fear for the future.

But Lot and his wife were adults. They were spiritually aware and understood that this was God's divine judgment. To look back signaled regret, connection, and longing for the way things were. And the way things were was pure evil. Some godly influence from being around Abraham all those years must have rubbed off on Lot. He knew instinctively what was behind him was not what his future should look like. He sheltered his children's eyes as they ran forward, looking straight ahead. Lot's wife, however, was tethered to the city's decadence.

Did you ever play tetherball as a child? The rope is tough and strong and refuses to let the ball go no matter how hard you hit it. When our heart is tethered to something or someone, it acts with the same stubbornness. Our hearts, for example, should be tethered to our spouses so that no matter what kind of adversity we are "hit" with, we will stay attached to each other. Lot's wife was tethered to the perversion and wickedness of Sodom. When she looked back, it was because the cord of lust for evil was stronger than her desire to be free.

My parents had gained spiritual wisdom throughout their lives. They understood some things about life I had no way of knowing as a youngster growing up. They protected me and sheltered me as much as possible from things they knew would draw me toward sin and rebellion against God. Why? Because they knew that those things would reach out their tentacles and attach themselves to my heart. One at a time, my heart and soul would become tethered to sin, and eventually, it would rule my life. I would then be doomed to constantly gaze back on those things to bring pleasure to my life.

A victorious life begins by staying free of all attachment to the things of this world. Don't believe the enemy when he says, "It's just this one time." That's a lie. Whether it's a drug, pornography, an affair, or even something as simple as a flirtatious glance, one time will not satisfy. You'll come back for another and another, each time allowing yourself to be entangled in the web of sin.

Jane and I have lived in the country for most of our adult life. Many mornings, we would come out of the front door, and the sun would catch a newly spun spider web just right, and it would look like it was made of diamonds. It was a beautiful sight. But by the afternoon, it had inevitably become the permanent home to several trapped insects. Some were still alive, but they could not free themselves no matter how much they struggled. That's how it is when you're trapped and tethered to sin.

What if you're already attached like Lot's wife? There's still hope. Like Lot and his children, you can stop looking and run in the opposite direction. Cover your eyes, turn off the computer, stop driving by her house, and do whatever you must to look the other way. Remember the Bible's advice? "Resist the devil, and he will flee from you" (James 4:7). The only way the insects trapped in that web could be free was for someone bigger and stronger than them to set them free. That is how you can get free. There is Someone who can set you free when you run to Him instead of toward sin.

> **Consider this: You cannot be nonchalant about the presence of sin in your life. Known rebellion against God is a cancer that will eat you alive. It requires surgery to remove it from your life. Cut it out, throw it away, and don't let it back in again. You can't do it alone. You will need God's help.**

"The focus of Satan's efforts is always
the same: to deceive us into believing
that the passing pleasures of sin are more
satisfying than obedience."

Sam Storms

This should be a very private moment for you. All of us have sin that plagues us and keeps us from the intimate relationship we'd like to have with God.

You may be comfortable writing them down or perhaps not. If these things are very private and the details might cause others pain and heartache, write them on a separate piece of paper.

Pray over them and ask God's forgiveness. Ask Him to give you victory over these sins in the future. Agree with Him that they are wrong.

Then, when you are done praying, take the paper and find a place to burn it safely. Every time you are tempted in the future, remind the enemy that those sins are forgiven and that God will give you the victory.

Who's In The Trees

Who's in the Trees

LISTENING TO GOD'S VOICE

I've always heard that listening is a learned skill. I think that's true. The problem is I'm still learning. I love to talk, and that's a problem when you're supposed to be listening. It's hard to speak and listen at the same time. Most of the time, we may feel that the person we're talking to may not have anything worthwhile to say. I know that sounds harsh. But isn't there at least a little truth in it?

But when it comes to listening to God, the whole dynamic changes. Nothing we say could ever be as important as what He has to say. And what He says is always worthwhile. One characteristic of God we rarely acknowledge is that He never speaks without purpose. There are no useless God-words. Every syllable is productive. Thus, we have Paul's instruction to Timothy: "All Scripture is God-breathed and is useful for teaching, rebuking, correcting and training in righteousness, so that the servant of God may be thoroughly equipped for every good work" (II Tim. 3:16-17 NIV).

While studying for a sermon in 2005, I was tuned in to God's "frequency." I was reading His Word, and that's when He usually speaks to me through the printed words on the page. But this time, God chose to speak out loud, at least to me. In short, God told me in no uncertain terms that we were to walk across the country to share our faith and pray for our nation. It was the beginning of the most faith-filled adventure of our lives. I was certain I heard Him. You have to be sure if you're going to undertake such a journey.

As a youth pastor, I found the most asked question was, "How can I know God's will?" When I sat behind the pastor's desk for many years, I found that adults tended to ask the same question. At the risk of oversimplifying my response to all of those inquiries, the truth is, what I basically said was, "You just have to listen." God speaks in a variety of ways: through His Word, through pastors and teachers, through books and devotionals, and sometimes out loud.

On one occasion in the Old Testament, God spoke another way: through rustling the leaves of the trees. That was David's signal to attack the Philistines.

> 23 So David inquired of the Lord, and he answered, "Do not go straight up, but circle around behind them and attack them in front of the poplar trees.
>
> 24 As soon as you hear the sound of marching in the tops of the poplar trees, move quickly, because that will mean the Lord has gone out in front of you to strike the Philistine army."
>
> 25 So David did as the Lord commanded him, and he struck down the Philistines all the way from Gibeon to Gezer.
>
> II Samuel 5:23-25

This is an intriguing story and one that should be talked about more. The victory at Jerusalem was a notable one (II Sam 5:6-10). The defeat of those who occupied the city would trigger several events which would shape the future of Israel. First, David would be anointed king of all of Israel (not just Judah), and Jerusalem would become the seat of power in the United Kingdom and later, in the Southern Kingdom after the nation was divided. The importance of this turning point in Jewish history cannot be overestimated.

When the Philistines heard that David was now king of all Israel, they gathered their forces and came after him. Evidently, they had long memories, and David's humiliating defeat of Goliath left quite a sour taste in their mouths. David exemplified a sensitive leader who refused to go into battle without God's clear direction. In some ways, this may have been counterintuitive for David. After all, he had many victories under his belt and defeated the best the Philistines had to offer with a sling and a few stones. Surely, he could take them with a whole army of men.

But David refused to do what many of us tend to do. He did not rely on his ability, battle record, or strength. He knew that victory, a real lasting victory, only comes when God wins the victory. He could have marched on, but he didn't. He could have moved forward, but instead, he stood still. He wasn't going forward until God said "go," and he wasn't going until God's specific plan was revealed to him. What self-control!

The plan for victory was unusual and different from what David would have done by instinct. Perhaps this is a good place for some godly wisdom: Your instinct, or as some people put it, your "gut," is not a reliable compass for accomplishing God's work. There is an overabundance of worldly wisdom that advises us to "follow our gut." Your feelings, emotions, desires, and preconceived notions can all be tied up in your gut, and those are not the best sources for godly guidance. Had David gone with this natural intuition, he likely would have suffered significant losses to his army and perhaps even defeat.

Instead, David asked the Lord for clear and specific guidance. And God answered his prayer, not with a general "go-that-a-way" finger point, but with direction on the path and the timing. The instructions were clear. One, don't attack them straight on; circle around and surprise them. Two, wait to move until you hear the sound of marching in the tops of the trees. David had to listen twice. Once to get the general directions and a second time to know the specific timing. David didn't rush off after the first word. He stuck around long enough to hear all that God had to say. And, of course, it ended in a great victory for Israel.

This was so important to us as we walked across America. We often faced the end of a section of Route 66 we were walking on and needed to know how to proceed. Sometimes, God said, "Go through the desert or walk on the Interstate." But there were also times when we needed to know the exact timing. We not only had to listen once or twice but constantly. If you want to know God's will, you must make a habit of listening to His voice.

> **Consider this: In order to hear God's voice, you must be able to recognize it. That means you must spend enough time in His presence to "know" what He sounds like. Just like a friend who calls, and you know who it is by the timbre and inflection of their voice. You should be so familiar with the Good Shepherd's voice that you are naturally drawn to Him as He speaks.**

"We often miss hearing God's voice
simply because we aren't paying
attention.

Rick Warren

As your final exercise, set aside at least 30 minutes of solitude to hear God's voice and set some goals for the future based on what you hear God say. You may want to write down your impressions here, but we encourage you to journal your conversations with God, including your goals and accomplishments. This can be a fantastic tool for encouraging you in the future.

Final Thoughts

Final Thoughts

Here are two true statements:

1. There is nothing better than living a life of faith.
2. There is nothing more difficult than living a life of faith.

Although you may wonder if both can be true simultaneously, you'll agree they can when you think about it. Here's why: Standing in faith can be really hard when the winds of popular opinion, peer pressure, and circumstance are blowing in the opposite direction. But nothing beats coming out on the other side of the fray, knowing that your faith stood firm. Everything around you may lie in ruin, but your faith stood the test of time.

Jane and I love all kinds of Christian music (neither of us thinks rap is music). We enjoy contemporary worship, Southern Gospel, 70s Jesus music, and both love hymns. One of my (Rick) favorite hymns is this one:

> Encamped along the hills of light,
>
> Ye Christian soldiers rise,
>
> And press the battle ere the night
>
> Shall veil the glowing skies; Against the foe in vales below
>
> Let all our strength be hurled;
>
> Faith is the victory, we know,
>
> That overcomes the world.
>
> Faith is the victory! Faith is the victory! O glorious victory,
>
> That overcomes the world.
>
> — Sankey and Yates

What I love about this hymn is that it teaches a vital principle for Christians who are serious about their faith. Here's the lesson: The victory is not in the victory. The victory is in having faith! Faith is the victory. Why is that important? Because if I have faith, I am never defeated, no matter the circumstances. It may look like defeat, devastation, disarray, or downright tragedy. But if my faith survives, it's a win.

That is terrific news! Because I cannot always control my circumstances, but I can have faith regardless of my situation. James admonishes first-century Christians for praying "amiss." We may often pray amiss when we pray for our circumstances to change. That's understandable; that's human nature. We don't enjoy pain and discomfort. No sane person does. But what we could pray, and maybe should pray, is that God will give us faith that stands despite our circumstances.

This book doesn't have all the answers. It doesn't solve the world's problems. It's probably full of things that others have already said. But it does contain truth. Truth that will help you live a faith-filled, victorious life, even in the toughest of times. Faith is a gift from God. So, ask your Heavenly Father for the kind of faith that perseveres, outlasts the circumstances, and stands when everything else around you falls.

A Favor to Ask

If you found this book helpful and encouraging, we would appreciate it so much if you would leave a rating and review wherever you purchased it. It helps others find the book and also encourages us as we continue to serve our Lord. You can also email or contact us through our website to let us know how this book helped you. Here's our contact information.

Rick and Jane McKinney

rickandjanemckinney@gmail.com

https://rickandjanemckinney.com

You can also find all of our other books on our website. Most are available in print and eBook format, and some in audiobooks. Thank you so much for reading our book. Blessings.

Rick and Jane McKinney

Things I learned while reading this book.

About the Authors

About the Authors

Rick and Jane McKinney

Rick and Jane McKinney have lived an extraordinary life of ministry. Once described as "mavericks," they have literally stepped out into the unknown to embrace God's call and have experienced His presence in a way that only comes through a life of obedience. Whether planting and pastoring churches, traveling the world to perform concerts, building a house in Mexico, traveling from village to village in India, or walking across America, they have followed His voice as He led them forward, one step at a time.

Both were raised in Christian homes and surrendered their lives to God's call long before they met. Jane's father was a church musician, and Rick's was a pastor. They met in the second week of their freshman year at Oklahoma Baptist University, fell in love, and have been a couple for over 50 years. Their commitment to God's leadership and each other has taken them on some unique and exciting journeys, the most unusual of which was their walk across America.

They both graduated with degrees in Church Music and have recorded four albums, performed hundreds of concerts, led worship in several churches, and written numerous Christian songs. Rick also has two Master's degrees, one in theology, one in Education, and a Doctor of Ministry degree. He now teaches at the University of the Cumberlands in Williamsburg, Kentucky. Jane teaches at the local high school.

Rick and Jane have three extraordinary children: Jared, Rebekah, and Shoshannah. All three excel in their respective fields.

They are passionate about Christ and hope their writing will inspire others to follow God's call on their lives.

Please use the next two pages to write down your impressions, revelations, lessons, or any thoughts you may have had while reading the book. Our prayer is that the truth contained within these pages will impact your life in a very powerful way.

If you'd like to know more of the story about the walk across America, you'll want to read, "And...So We Walked: The Inspirational Story of a Couple's Walk Across America."

Here's an excerpt from the book:

The emergency room was complete with bright lights, doctors and nurses in scrubs and stainless-steel trays with long hypodermic needles. Some of the medical staff were poking and prodding their way around in examination while others rolled their portable machines in and out of the cramped room. It was remarkably like a scene on television. The weeping wife was the most difficult thing to see, worried more than anyone would ever know about the patient who lay on the emergency room stretcher. Watching her brought tears to the husband's eyes as he struggled to reassure her by clenching her hand in his.

What made this scene different from any I'd seen before, even when I had been summoned to emergency rooms as a pastor, was seeing it all happen from the patient's perspective. It was all happening to me. The patient they were examining was me. The hospital wristband had my name on it and this time, my wife was standing there.

I could hear the emergency room doctor carrying on a phone conversation with the Burn Center at the desk just across the hall from my room. He was talking about me. Fighting back the urge to close my eyes and sleep, I strained to hear what he was saying but could only catch a few words here and there. Now a different doctor, an orthopedic surgeon, had entered the overcrowded quarters and was pulling and tugging on my left index finger. Although he was pulling hard enough to make him grimace, the Lidocaine, administered in five or six shots had done its job and I could only feel some slight pressure

Ever since I was hospitalized at age seven to have my tonsils removed, I had never been able to smell the distinct mixture of hospital aromas without feeling nauseated. I couldn't tell if the smell, the drugs, or the trauma caused me to feel as though I might pass out, but I struggled to stay awake.

The emergency room doctor was off the phone now and a conference was happening in the hall just outside my room. They broke their huddle and came alongside my temporary bed. "Mr. McKinney, I just got off the phone with the Burn Center in Little Rock and we've decided the best thing is to go ahead and transfer you there right now," the man in the white coat and stethoscope said with no emotion. It was the last thing I wanted to hear, but before it could sink in the orthopedic surgeon took his turn. "I was able to put your dislocated finger back into place, but I'm not sure what kind of function you will have. It was a severe injury. There is a good chance you will need surgery to repair it later, but your burns are the primary concern right now. We will put your finger in a splint and give you some instructions for taking care of it. Before we transfer you, do you have any questions?"

Did I have any questions? Only a couple of dozen like, "How long will I be off my feet?" or "Will this stop our walk across America?" or "Did I hear something about skin grafts?" or "Will I ever be able to play the piano again?" But as those questions were racing through my mind, only one was critical. Only one question was going to make any real difference. Only one question would come out of my mouth. I looked as intently as I could at the doctor and tried to shake off the effects of the morphine. "Just one," I said, "just one...."

Available on Kindle in Paperback, Kindle, and Audiobook.

www.ingramcontent.com/pod-product-compliance
Lightning Source LLC
Chambersburg PA
CBHW020902090426
42736CB00008B/462